Made In Reality

Stephanie Pratt

Made In Reality

<u>headline</u>

The right of Stephanie Pratt to be identified as the Author of
the Work has been asserted by her in accordance with the
Copyright, Designs and Patents Act 1988.

First published in 2015
by HEADLINE PUBLISHING GROUP

1

Cataloguing in Publication Data is available from the British Library

Hardback ISBN 978 1 4722 3034 8

Typeset in Berling by Palimpsest Book Production Limited,
Falkirk, Stirlingshire

Printed and bound in Great Britain by Clays Ltd, St Ives plc

Headline's policy is to use papers that are natural, renewable
and recyclable products and made from wood grown in
sustainable forests. The logging and manufacturing
processes are expected to conform to the environmental
regulations of the country of origin.

MIX
Paper from
responsible sources
FSC
www.fsc.org FSC® C104740

HEADLINE PUBLISHING GROUP
An Hachette UK Company
Carmelite House
50 Victoria Embankment
London EC4 0DZ

www.headline.co.uk
www.hachette.co.uk

For my parents, who not only gave me life, but taught me its value. You never gave up on me, even when I tried to give up on myself.

Contents

Foreword

'It's just that the Fourth of July is coming up, and, well . . . there are going to be a lot of pool parties.'

I looked down at the grass of Kristin's backyard where I was sitting. I could still see the crew inside her Hollywood home, packing up after our final day of filming. Kristin, Lo and Audrina, who had been friends and co-stars on the show for years now, were inside, chatting. So close I could hear them laugh.

'And I don't want you to be worried . . .' he continued, '. . . because there might be, you know, photos.'

Hang on. What was happening here? Keep it cool, Stephanie.

'That's cool, babe, have a great time,' I said. But I was starting to wonder where this conversation was going. We had finished filming the final episode of *The Hills* that day,

1

and now my boyfriend was calling me, and sounding weird.

'They're in Vegas.'

'Oka-ay.'

'So, you know, I might not always be able to call you to say goodnight.'

'What?'

'It's just, things . . . well, they're all a bit serious.'

'What do you mean they're serious? We live together!'

We did. Josh Hansen had been my boyfriend for six months now. We shared my LA home, he spent time with my family, and we had talked about getting married. Only a week ago we had filmed my 'happy ever after' ending for *The Hills*, with him on his cross-bike, training, and us committing to each other seriously. He had become a cast member for this series. And now he was saying that things were all a bit serious?

'Yeah, I know, but, like, it's about to be summer and there are going to be so many great parties, like, everywhere,' he said.

'What are you getting at?' I asked. This whole conversation was galloping away from me now. I was starting to see where it was going and I didn't like it one little bit.

'I don't think I can do this,' he replied.

'Right. Which pool party is it that you need to be single for?' I asked, my heart in my mouth. Who was the girl he might be photographed with?

'There's not one in particular,' he said. 'I'm just assuming that there's going to be a bunch.'

Great. So he's breaking up with me for a potential pool party that doesn't even exist, for a new girlfriend he hasn't even met yet.

Lo came outside and saw that I had tears streaming down my face, silently. I was just staring at my phone wondering how that conversation had just happened. This wasn't some guy I'd met in a club, or someone I had dated a few times because it might get me attention in the show, or the papers. He was, I thought, a really good boyfriend. He would play princesses with my little niece. We hung out together in private as much as in public and I had never been happier.

Lo put her arm around me, and lifted my face to look at hers.

'Josh just broke up with me for potential pool parties on the Fourth of July,' I said.

'Er, what?' she said, dumbfounded.

But she was the one who put two and two together the fastest.

'So now the show's over he doesn't want to know. He's a piece of shit.'

Suddenly, it became clear. He did really enjoy being on camera. He had always hung around a lot, chatting to the crew . . . So Josh would befriend them, bigging up his life as a motocross rider.

'We've got to get you guys down to the track some

time,' I had heard him tell them. But I didn't care that he was stepping into my on-screen world. I knew it would work. When you're on these shows, everyone is always looking for something new to film. A new location, something dynamic, a fresh view on LA. Us girls were always gossiping in cafés so this was a fantastic change for everyone. A dirt track, watching him do jumps, then him coming over to kiss me.

I mean, swoon.

He was my soulmate, and him being on *The Hills* would just make me look cool. Stephanie Pratt and her super-hot boyfriend on a motorbike.

It was working out for everyone.

Except now, I hadn't been done with *The Hills* for more than five minutes – I was still in the same clothes and make-up! – yet I was expendable.

'How did I not see this?' I said in despair.

'Because he lived with you, he hung out with your family. He seemed to love you.'

Lo was right. He had done a good job of convincing me he was 'the one'.

The reality is that there's always a fresh way to get your heart broken. I might have thought that the best make-up, the best soundtrack and the best lighting would have protected me from that, but I was wrong.

The show was over but the drama carried on. I was still in my filming make-up as I packed all of Josh's stuff into the back of my car and drove it round to the apartment of the friend who had introduced us.

As I looked in the mirror that night, my face finally bare, I took a moment to look at the 'real' me. Was it the TV me that Josh had wanted, or was there still something in there that was loveable, without the cameras?

In the next few weeks, Josh kept calling me, saying he wanted to talk. He tried to get himself invited to Lauren Conrad's Fourth of July party, where I had a great time with my friends. I had seen what his reality was, and sure enough it turned out that the calls were because he just wanted me to attend the X Games with him for PR. I went, because he gave me a story about how he needed me there or he might mess up, but he left for the after-party without me.

When I got to the party, Kelly Osbourne came up to me and gave me a huge hug.

'I heard what happened,' she said. 'I'm so sorry. Josh is the worst, such a total dickhead. Sleep on it tonight – just keep hanging out with us, you can do so much better, forget about him.'

One week later – one! – I look at Perez Hilton's website and see an article about Kelly Osbourne and Josh Hansen on a date. Part of me was glad to have made up my mind that this guy was good for nothing, but most of me just felt heartbroken to have been taken in in the first place.

The Hills might have been over, but my life, as ever, was turning out to be more real than reality itself.

1

There was no reality TV when I was growing up. TV was MTV, *Baywatch* and *Saved by the Bell*. Celebrity was a by-product, not an industry, and when you're growing up in Hollywood it is a by-product that is not in short supply. Everyone has a story, and here's mine . . .

I was born on 11 April 1986 but I think my story began a few years earlier, at a restaurant called Trancas. My parents were on a blind date, set up by my aunt, and it was love at first sight. It was the 1980s, it was Malibu, and everything was perfect.

My mom Janet was a ski instructor in one of the ski resorts in Mammoth, California. She had a small daughter, my sister Kristin, and she had just divorced from her high-school sweetheart. Meanwhile my aunt, who already had a boyfriend, had spotted that a new single man had moved into her residential area. It was my dad, William. At first she thought he was just a sort of surfer guy who had turned up with his blue Porsche and his tan. He was actually a dentist with a roster of celebrity clients.

'Janet, you have to come and meet my new neighbour,' she told my mom. 'I will babysit Kristin, just get yourself down here.'

'Tell me more . . .' said my mom, and soon she was sold on the promise of a surfing dentist with a kind heart and a good tan.

The date took place the next weekend. Trancas was a beachfront restaurant where bands like Fleetwood Mac would play, overlooking the ocean. It must have been the most romantic first date ever, and from that moment on they were inseparable. They got married in a church in Santa Monica not long afterwards, and had their reception at The Beach Club. They have now been married for thirty years and they're still obsessed with each other, the cutest couple ever. My dad was as he is now – relaxed, non-confrontational, the guy who sorts everything out without making a fuss. And my mom has always been a sunny, smiley personality – but the one who worries about us all too.

Mind you, there was not too much to make a fuss about back then. We had the ultimate relaxing beach childhood. My mom had an easy pregnancy and even met her best

8

friend Lucy while they were in beds next to each other in the maternity ward. They were both having boys, two days apart, and were like blonde Californian twins. They have stayed pals ever since, and it was only three years before I appeared on the scene, ready for a bit of the Californian action.

My first appearance in the press came the week I was born. The *Malibu Times* featured my birth in its 'Storkistics' column, saying 'Welcome to Malibu, Stephanie', and the *Malibu Surfside News* also carried an announcement.

My mom found out she was having a girl in her fourth month of pregnancy, and the whole family was thrilled, especially ten-year-old Kristin who was ecstatic to have a baby sister to play with. Apparently I kicked a lot but would always stop when my dad put his hand on my mom's tummy. Mine was a natural birth with no medication at all, and I was soon nicknamed Peanut by most of the family – apart from Spencer who was coming up to three and could only say 'Weffie'.

Not much has changed with my brother since we were kids. He was always a charismatic child – there was never a dull moment. If you walked by the park and saw kids playing in the sandpit, he'd always be at the centre of it, making sure the sandcastle was being built right. He always had tons of friends, and there was always lots of laughter around him. He really knew from day one how to love life. He was involved in every sport, and was always there at the pizzeria afterwards eating and laughing with the team. I always just thought he was so cool, so much fun, even if he was always playing pranks on me. There was always a new magic trick, or some ruse where I would get tied up and made to escape. It was non-stop shenanigans, non-stop winding my parents up and it was always the best fun to be on his side watching the mayhem take place.

Kristin wasn't around so much because she was ten years older than me. By the time I can remember her she was already a mysterious teenager with her own life. It all seemed impossibly glamorous and rebellious to me. I remember one story about her taking her braces off which seemed so naughty! And another time she sneaked out of the house at night as she had her own staircase from her bedroom leading directly out to the backyard. She seemed so fearless, she even went to raves!

I suspect that I may have massively exaggerated all of this to myself. Maybe Kristin only went out once and it just made a huge impact on me. I was such a goody-two-shoes that this kind of scandal blew my mind back then. The fact is, I just wanted everyone to be happy all the time. We didn't grow up around conflict, it really wasn't part of our lives. Every year our Christmas photos are just smiles and laughter. There were no adults fighting downstairs at night, no edge to family discussions, nothing. Back then, life really was just one long day at the beach.

Malibu is just outside of Los Angeles, it is an entirely

coastal spot, just a few shops and houses along the beach. It wasn't a movie-industry kind of a place back then. It was like a little village, where everyone knew everyone else. A birthday party wasn't a hired-out club or a load of entertainers, it was just some pony rides along the beach. The stores along the seafront or at the Country Mart didn't used to be chic designer names or organic bistros back in the 1980s and 1990s, it was trinket stores. You couldn't buy light-diffusing blusher or vine-ripened tomatoes, but you could get buckets and spades, surfboards and bathing suits galore! If you wanted more than a bikini back then, you had to head into LA, but at that point in my life Hollywood seemed far away, just a place where Dad's work contacts were.

Celebrity wasn't a big deal to us. Famous people were just 'Dad's clients' a lot of the time. He had his own dentistry practice in Santa Monica with some big-name clients who he saw in a vulnerable position because of his job. No one likes going to the dentist, so his easygoing manner and way of treating celebrities like normal people meant that he built up a great business and made sure we were aware that they were just living, breathing human beings. I didn't want to be famous back then – what was the point? I just wanted to be a national horseback rider.

Horses were my obsession. And if it wasn't horses it was reading. If I could be reading about horses, so much the better! When I was eight I was even given a pony for

Christmas. It was the best day of my life, and sometimes I think it still is. A pony! The entire family was in on the surprise – I was told we were driving to my grandparents for Christmas dinner and on the way there my mom took a detour. We pulled up in a little field and there were my dad, Spencer and Kristin with Kiwi my pony, who was wearing a huge red and white bow. I couldn't believe it, I was weeping with excitement while Spencer was just goofing around saying, 'How do you tell this thing to "sit"? It's huge . . .'

It may sound cheesy, but that is just one example of what was genuinely a dream childhood for me. It seemed inconceivable that I could go on to live a life defined by drama and conflict for so many years. How could I cope with that if I had had so little experience of it growing up? Well, maybe that was the problem . . .

When I was about five the family moved along the coast from Malibu to the Pacific Palisades area of Los Angeles. The Palisades is a quiet countryside area, albeit one that is peppered with the homes of huge celebrities. It is a really small spot though, and in the 1990s it was still the kind of place where you didn't lock your door at night. Every house is a perfect house with a perfect family in it. There's no random government housing or crime that might spoil the image of the area. It's wealth, it's peace, it's boring. It's the kind of place where everything shuts at 9.00 pm and you have to go to neighbouring Santa Monica, where LA properly begins, if you even want to find a bar.

By the time I entered high school I was surrounded by the children of celebrities, and indeed a few future celebrities. Spencer and I attended the now notorious Crossroads School in Santa Monica. A private school, it is the sort of place that makes *Clueless* look like a documentary because of its stereotypical LA behaviours and celebrity kids – we had classmates such as Jonah Hill and previous students were Kate Hudson and Zooey Deschanel. Consequently, I was seeing flashbulbs popping in and around Los Angeles since I was about ten and it didn't frighten me, nor did it really impress me. It was how some people live, but as my dad always told me, they were all human and that was that. Nevertheless I was aware of what fame was – and what it could bring.

My first understanding of what a celebrity was had taken place when I was about eight. My best friend at that time was Meryl Streep's daughter. I knew her mom was different from my mom . . . but she was still just a mom. She took us to see *Fiddler on the Roof* one evening and we were so excited to see the show. But what I hadn't anticipated and really didn't understand was when she was stopped by the press on the way in. Everyone noticed her and wanted to ask her questions, but I was only eight so the most I thought was that 'Gracie's mom is really funny.'

When I was about thirteen I took some acting lessons, as pretty much all young teens in Hollywood do at some point. I really enjoyed them, but I suspect it was more as an avenue for self-expression and getting those teenage hormones off my chest! Then at around fourteen I was 'discovered' outside of school and offered my first modelling job. I couldn't believe it, I had only had my braces off that month and already I was being asked to model – how thrilling! And boy did I hit the big time with that gig – I was on the cardboard packet for a set of fake fingernails. Superstardom! Lol!

Things were still pretty grounded for a while yet though. My mom was a stay-at-home mom and my dad drove us to school every day on the way to his dental practice. I loved high school and until my teens I was happy, sociable and having a great time. When I wasn't at school it was ballet classes, swim lessons, gymnastics, volleyball and pottery. My pottery phase was immense – I was always making little handcrafted gifts for Kristin! My other love was soccer. I kept up soccer all the way into high school – it was up there with horses for a while. Little did I know how useful it would prove to be in the future as an honorary Brit, and one with a Brit boyfriend . . .

Despite the soccer I was still a really girly girl in matters of style. I spent years trying to dress in matching outfits to my mom or sister. Kristin adored me and treated me as a sort of practice run for her own kids. I thrived on the attention and we have always had a great relationship. I loved wearing make-up, frilly clothes, anything lacy or satin, and refused to wear jeans for years as a child because they 'didn't look pretty'.

At school, it was all about reading – and science club. Seriously, I had a wonderful time at science club, and got along great with all the guys there. All of my friends were boys at that age. From the age of seven until about ten or eleven I was completely used to dealing with boys because of the mayhem that Spencer and his friends brought with them. I had spent years stepping around him and my dad fake wrestling on the living-room floor or listening to him winding me up, so I wasn't as intimidated by the boys at school as some girls who hadn't grown up around them were. I adored Spencer, even though he was now starting to get into a bit of trouble with his cheeky ways. So, having boys around seemed entirely relaxed to me, a part of normal life, not a source of potential future boyfriends – and if they got a bit much, I always had my books. My reading choices were *Goosebumps* or the *Sweet Valley High* books, or anything Judy Blume did – as well as the horsey books of course.

It was seventh grade, when I was around twelve, that things started to change. Sixth grade is when a lot of primary schools end, so our larger school accepted quite a few kids from nearby schools in LA for the next school year. This included a large intake of girls from a very 'cool' school in Santa Monica called Wildwood. I had been the girl who was obsessed with science club and her pony when suddenly girls in my class started to turn up in padded bras, with Celine handbags. I had been a naive little girl for my first few years at middle school, one of the guys, but now they'd become interested in girls . . .

Within a week I became invisible to the boys I had grown up with and silently started nursing crushes on. Effectively, I became a boy, just someone the guys could ask to pass a note to the girl they had a crush on. The budding flirtations I had started to enjoy while I had the full attention of the gang had now changed to little more than 'Oh, could you ask Roxy if she can meet me at the Brentwood Country Mart later?' Great.

It seemed like a case of fitting in or losing out. I had to get to grips with make-up and fashion. These girls were kids whose dads were largely players in the movie or music industry so they knew what they were talking about. I was buying more and more magazines every week, getting to know the models I did and didn't like, and the styles I did and didn't want to copy. Suddenly I knew who Kate Spade was and what a Prada handbag looked like. But I also knew what a plummeting sense of self-esteem felt like, and the more I flicked through the pages of *Vogue*, the more I lost sight of who I really was.

It was fun for a year or so, it really was. And these girls did become good friends. We shared all sorts of firsts like putting colour in our hair (my mom was heartbroken), experimenting with those little rhinestone tattoos that were so big in the 1990s and of course talking about boys. I was self-conscious that I didn't have my first kiss for years after some of my new friends, but managed to hide that fact by bonding with them in other ways. In the end, at the beginning of ninth grade, I was on a mission to get it over with and I just kissed a sixteen-year-old called Jessie Israel outside a house party in his SUV. 'Argh, finally, it's done!' was my main thought. The pressure kept on building at the back of my mind though: look good, be cool, keep up.

Me, Courtney, Z, Claire and Roxy were soon a proper little clique, sitting together in classes, phoning each other in the evenings and hanging out together on the weekends ordering pizza and going to the pool to tan all together. We would talk about celebrities and fashion for hours, my head suddenly filled with their parents' industry-insider gossip. I was part of the Wildwood Girls' gang and I was determined to stay one.

We loved nothing more than 'being fancy', and basically this involved trying to copy what we saw the adults around us doing. We would go to Neiman Marcus with the Visa Buxx our parents had given us. These were credit cards for kids, which had a $400 limit and our parents had to sign for to say the purchases would be covered by them. We would head there together, thinking we looked like something from *Sex and the City*, except our designer handbags would be entirely empty apart from that one card and our clunky early Nokia phones – as we were kids we didn't need anything else! We would spend hours shopping for the latest must-have item – Miu Miu platforms, for example

– and then have to coordinate via phone that night to make sure that we all wore them on the same day.

Wherever we heard our parents were going for dinner, we would try and go for lunch. We would head off together like a mini version of *Real Housewives*. Those Visa Buxx cards were emptied every month. Everywhere we went, everyone was lovely to us, because they knew we had those cards, and they knew who the adults providing them were. I had everything I wanted back then, and if I could have asked for a single thing more it would have been 'to be a grown-up'.

If only I had known what growing up too fast was going to feel like, I am sure I would have tried to postpone it rather than do the reverse. Because if you get depressed when everything is perfect, growing up becomes the hardest thing of all to do.

2

It wasn't too long before the increasing sense that teen life wasn't just fun shopping and fancy lunches started to overwhelm me. Admittedly, I was having an extreme teen experience with all the beauty and the wealth that Los Angeles has in such abundance laid out in front of me. But it still felt like too much alongside all of the changes that were happening in my own body. I went from having a school satchel to a handbag that cost $200 so fast that I could barely keep up.

A sort of depression started to wind its tentacles around my mind. I felt down all of the time, instead of being the happy, sunny girl everyone knew. Nothing seemed to be able to make me happy any more, and as I tried to keep up with the social pressures I was under, my concentration started to suffer too. I just found it harder and harder to be myself.

It was not long after these feelings began that I was diagnosed with Attention-Deficit Disorder (ADD). It shouldn't have been a big deal, as at that point in the mid-1990s almost everyone was being diagnosed with it. All the moms were saying, 'Oh God, I'd better get my kid tested, there's a new thing out there that might be harming her.' It often began if we weren't concentrating when we were in class – and I certainly wasn't a lot of the time. I was off staring into space, distracted by almost anything. But then, so are a lot of kids, especially teenagers living in a city like Los Angeles where distractions can be so extreme.

Basically, it seemed anyone can have ADD. You could find the symptoms if you were in a bad place and you wanted to sort things out fast. I know my mom and my doctor wanted to help, but at that point my diagnosis reinforced the idea that I had imperfections all of a sudden.

It wasn't hard for me to get diagnosed, and – pow! – just like that I had extra time in all my tests as well as being given a prescription for pills called Adderall. These days, we all know a bit more about the drug – how addictive it is, how it can affect people in the long run and the other countless problems that the press have picked up on. Nowadays, it seems more people are inclined to look at diet, or therapy, than just to take the pills. Diet, exercise and therapy are certainly what I would recommend as a starting point these days!

I'm not sure why, but Adderall had the strange effect of making me feel more depressed than ever before. I had gone from happy to anxious and then instead of returning to my previous happy self, I had slumped into a seemingly unending sadness that I could never really get a grip on. The drug was meant to slow my fidgety mind, but it seemed to make me way too flat. I had always been goofy and smiley but now I was a dark person.

I kept up appearances on the outside like a good Californian teenager but inside I stayed so, so low and I had no idea why. My parents, bless them, only wanted to help, and arranged for me to visit different therapists to try and get to the bottom of this feeling of never-ending flatness. It was on the way to one of those appointments that I made one of the biggest mistakes of my life.

I had been hanging out with a girl, Nicole, who was a year or two older than me. She was in love with Spencer, and was desperate to get his attention, so she made it her business to befriend me. She started to give me a lot of time. I could not believe my luck. She had a Lexus, and she would give me lifts all over LA – we'd go to Barneys Department Store, or to get our nails done together after school. Of course I thought she was the coolest person ever. For my insecure, would-be fabulous self she was the best thing that had ever happened to me.

Except she wasn't. One sunny afternoon we went to Country Mart in Brentwood together – it's a little group of chic restaurants and boutiques, a sort of deluxe mini-mall, where you always end up seeing celebrities being photographed. We had just had some lunch and she was about to drop me off at my next therapist's appointment.

As we sat in the Lexus she pulled out a small glass pipe and started fiddling with it.

'What is that?' I asked.

'Oh, it's like Adderall,' she replied. 'Isn't that what you take? Do you want some?'

'Is it speed?' I asked. 'Because my mom says I can never ever take anything like that as I have a heart murmur, and I'll drop dead.'

'Well, you're already taking Adderall,' she reasoned. 'This is basically just melting that and smoking it like a cigarette.'

She was older than me, she was wiser than me, and the Adderall wasn't doing much that felt like speed anyway, so I couldn't really see a problem with it.

'Do you swear to God it's not speed?' I repeated, just in case. 'Because I will drop dead and it'll be your fault.'

I watched her take the glass pipe with the bowl and long tube and put some little crystals in it. She melted them with a lighter, then she took the flame away and all the melted liquid froze on to the inside of the glass bowl part of the pipe. Then she took a hit of it, breathing in the smoke; she re-melted it and then inhaled the smoke again. You couldn't smell a thing. There was no fragrance at all from any of it, no toxic fumes, so it didn't seem too bad. Curiosity beyond curiosity was burning up in me. I was with an older girl who had just told me it was a fun cool way of taking medication I was already on. What's not to like, I reasoned.

She passed the pipe to me. I took a hit, like a dumdum, but I didn't feel anything at all. I had tried weed once or twice before and it had always given me a huge, instant head rush. It smells, you can feel it on the back of your throat, and then you get that rush – you know that some-thing is happening. But with this, there was just a puff of white smoke and nothing else.

'Well, I need to do it again, I didn't feel anything,' I said. And I kept on and on wanting to do it, wanting to feel something, saying, 'It's broken, it's not working for me.'

All she said was, 'Wow, you are going to be so high.'

Great friend.

Half an hour later I was sitting in the therapist's room, discussing my body image issues. As so often with teenage girls, those looking to help had seen it as a necessary part of my therapy to deal with my low moods. But this time, instead of engaging with the issues, I was mostly just scratching my forehead wildly. I really couldn't stop. It was my first meeting with this therapist, and understandably it did not take her long to ask me if I had done drugs.

'Oh my God, no!!' I replied, outraged. My Adderall was a prescription drug after all! I didn't miss a beat, then carried on rattling through whatever it was I had to say. All the while, I continued to pick apart my forehead, just for something to do.

Again she asked about drugs. This time it was, 'Have you ever heard of speed bumps?' Again I said no. She explained that speed bumps are when people who have taken drugs feel like they have bugs on them, and that makes them scratch at their face and arms. I was so high, and not even aware that I was high, so I had no idea that I was displaying exactly this behaviour. I didn't have a clue what she was talking about. Why was she telling me this?

After therapy Nicole picked me up to take me home. She gave me a little bit of a hit and we went and bought me a pipe at a tobacco shop on Santa Monica Boulevard on the way back. I felt confident, I felt like I was a super-model. I had been so depressed before, for so long, and suddenly I felt alive again. I felt so happy. I was on cloud nine, it was the best drug in the entire world.

Within a couple of weeks, and without me ever noticing it, I was in the grips of a full-blown addiction. The crystal meth – because that is what it was, despite me not real-ising for a while – had become my coping strategy, my life. I got thinner, I felt better with my body image. As the weeks and then months rolled by, I became the thin-nest girl in school, and that was always the goal in LA.

For so long, it was impossible to find any negatives with my new situation.

I would wake up, and pop out of bed because I was so excited to take my meth. No more teen surliness for me. For months the alarm had gone off and my only thought had been 'Urgh'. Now, I jumped out of bed. I'd go into my bathroom and smoke, immediately, then brush my teeth, put on my make-up and get dressed. Then I would get in my car. Yeah, I'd get in my car. High. Sometimes I would be desperate enough that I would be at a red light and during that pause I would bend down and smoke it in the driver's seat. At the wheel.

Then I'd get to school and park underneath the supermarket across the road from school. I would sit in the car and do it again. Then I'd put it back in my little Hello Kitty bag that I kept all my kit in, and put it in the armrest of the car, get out of the parking lot and head for school. About half the time I would get to the outside of the supermarket and then turn around and walk back into the garage. I would get everything out of the Hello Kitty bag again and do some more, before heading for school a second time. It would be 8.10 am and I would have smoked meth four times already. At least.

Now I can see how completely mad it all sounds. But then, as far as I was concerned, there were no disadvantages. Sure, once I had actually made it to school, I was completely forgetful. I would turn up without my backpack and have to go back to the car for a third time. I must have looked crazy. But no one cared. Teenage girls are so self-involved that they didn't even notice anything. They were all texting, playing with their hair and worrying about their own stuff. Plus, I remained a pleasure to be around. I was friends with everyone in school by this point. My Neiman Marcus make-over had been a total success, and I believed my body-image worries were gone forever. I never had enemies because I was just so happy all of the time. I certainly didn't have the ability to be malicious by that point.

The forgetfulness was off the scale, though. On occasion I would be walking back to my car, hunting in my bag for my keys and starting to freak out that they weren't in there. I'd reach the car and see that the keys were in the ignition, and the car was on. And it had been like that for five or six hours.

Within weeks I was going to all sorts of sketchy places to get the meth, meeting crazy dealers at storage facilities and parking lots. There was a trailer next to a car wash with a guy in it called Jason. It really was the cliché. I want to say this sounds like something out of *Breaking Bad* but I can't ever, ever watch that show, because even watching someone using that drug on screen takes me back to such a dark place. I hate that I ever did it; it gives me shivers to be reminded.

It took more than a year before it finally looked as if the game was up. I was seventeen and the size of a child. My forearms, all around my collarbone and my shoulders were covered in tiny scabs where I had picked and picked at myself. Appropriately enough on Halloween 2002, I was called in by one of the teachers and told that they 'just wanted to make sure everything was okay with me'. The school therapist was in the room, too.

'What are you talking about?!' was my response.

'Some of the girls have come in and expressed concern about your appearance and what it might mean,' she replied. 'You have lost some weight and you are missing a lot of class.'

'Yeah, well I'm trying to diet. I am signed with LA Models, you know,' I said. (That one false nails packaging ad had come via LA Models when I was fourteen.)

I told them other girls were just envious, and I stuck to my story.

'How dare they. Those jealous bitches,' I said about the classmates who had clearly shown concern for their friend. None of them knew what I was really smoking, as I had always maintained that it was hash oil, and never let anyone touch any of the kit in my Hello Kitty bag, ever. It was super-mean of me to speak about them like that, as people were obviously genuinely worried. But I knew what it took to defend myself in the high school environment. Or so I thought.

I was freaking out inside though. I suppose I was high when they called me in, because I was always high, but I had my game face on when I was on that drug. After all, that was why I took it – it worked for me.

'You can ask my teachers. My grades could not be better,' I spat at them.

I knew I wasn't far off because I was up all night getting my work in, getting extra credits – fuelled with surplus energy to get the homework done by being high.

'Just because I have lost weight there is nothing to be concerned about. I won't tolerate other girls' envy.' I turned on my heel and left.

The minute I got out of that meeting I knew I had to get to my mom before they did. I was in my Halloween costume, driving home – high – and I called her as fast as I could.

'Oh my God, Mom, the school has called me up, they've all ganged up on me, the others in class have become jealous and been saying the most disgusting things about me.'

My mom felt terrible for me and gave me lots of sympathy. Nailed it. It was safe to go home. She would still be on my side even if the school did call her to give their version of the meeting. I had gotten there first, suckers! When I got home Mom gave me a huge hug and told me everything would be fine.

By Thanksgiving, it would be a different story.

That weekend I was at my best friend Roxy's house. The usual group of girls was hanging out together, having a sleep over. We were downstairs in the living room and as the evening wore on Roxy's mom went to bed. All afternoon, and then all evening, I had kept popping upstairs to the bathroom to smoke some more meth. I guess it was about every forty minutes or so, and each time I went, I had to pass Roxy's mom's bedroom. I'm sure she would have expected a fair bit of clanking around in the bathroom if she had a house full of teenage girls spending the night, but it seems that the regularity and frequency of my trips meant that I had specifically caught her attention.

I had no idea that anyone was keeping an eye out for me though, and carried on just as I usually did. Loving life, for as long as I could sneak out to smoke some more meth at regular intervals. In hindsight, this was naive of me. Roxy's mom must have been keen to check up on me. Quite apart from the fact that the faculty and other students clearly knew that something was up, even if they had yet to catch me in the act, there must have been gossip going on about me among the parents too. My folks were friends with a lot of my friends' parents, and my mom and brother especially had been vigorous in defending me if anyone started to 'spread gossip' within their earshot.

Everyone was still so ignorant about what meth was back then though – myself included. My ever more regular meetings with dealers meant that I knew it couldn't all be good, but I was still under the impression that this was essentially a harmless recreational drug. I would never have let myself get involved with something gnarly at this point.

29

After all, only a few years ago I had been the kid making pottery signs that said DRUGS with a massive cross striking through the letters. Weirdly, I still saw myself as essentially anti-drugs.

When Claire and Roxy headed to bed, we all had a laugh about the fact that I wouldn't be getting my head down for a good few hours more. It had become a standing joke that I just never slept. They knew I was on something, but still I persisted with telling them that it was hash oil and they wouldn't like it. I loved my best friends like sisters and I would never introduce them or anyone to meth. I had been tricked into it, and now it controlled my life. I wasn't going to let it take any more prisoners. I think Claire and Roxy suspected it wasn't hash oil but they never asked me too many questions. Looking back I think they were scared. They didn't want to know what was in that Hello Kitty bag that made me act and look so different. So I continued down the dark hole alone. As long as my friends were safe from meth it could do whatever it wanted to me.

The other strange thing about nights like these – but especially this one – is that I cannot for the life of me remember what I would be doing when the others fell asleep. Obviously I would still be making my frequent trips to the bathroom, but apart from that I have no idea. It was a time before smartphones or social media, so the mindless time-wasting that I can do now with just my phone and an Instagram feed wasn't an option in those days. I suppose there were some magazines and maybe I would have the TV on in the room, but it seems incredible to me now that I could have wasted all of that time. What was I staying awake for? Just to experience a bit more of the sensation of being high? I suppose it must have been that, as there is no other real aim that I have any recollection of at all. I only remember thinking that it was fun, so much fun.

How much fun could it have been though? I was by now spending all of my pocket money on it, hundreds of dollars a month, and the pleasure it gave me seems so limited when I look back on it. It was totally antisocial, as I wasn't sharing doing it with my friends, but was having to build up a network of dealers and other addicts to keep me supplied at all times. It was as if I had access to a whole other world, and they really weren't the kind of people I would otherwise have chosen to have in my life. When you embark on something like this you realise how many other people are on that journey too – you just never notice it if you're not a part of that world.

I was scared of the dealers because they seemed so paranoid, always looking into their mirrors checking for cops and wanting to get you in and out as fast as they could. They often wanted to meet and drive around the block which inevitably raised the possibility that they could just drive off anywhere with me in the vehicle. From this one girl, Nicole, I now had a whole universe of shady people in my life, and it was becoming increasingly clear that my secret life, the one I was hiding from friends and family, was becoming my real life. Or at least the one I was spending the most time living.

No matter how little I can remember of what I did that Saturday night at Roxy's, the Sunday morning that followed it will be etched on my memory forever. I woke up, feeling fine, had a little smoke, then left Roxy's and headed home. When I got back I saw my dad in the kitchen, and asked him if he wanted to head out and get sandwiches with me in a while.

'Yeah, just give me a minute,' he said. He seemed distracted, less than his usual cheery self.

When I started walking upstairs I realised why.

'GET IN HERE NOW' My brother Spencer had walked down the stairs to meet me and was pointing upstairs, his face clouded with rage.

What the hell?

Spencer was holding a can of Dr Pepper soda and pointing in the direction of my parents' bedroom. I followed him up, walking as slowly as I could, dreading what might be coming my way. But I had bluffed my way through this once, I figured I could do it again if I needed to . . .

It was nearly midday, very unusual for my mom to still be in bed, but as I turned the corner into their room I saw her there, sitting in bed sobbing. She was devastated, as if someone had just died. I opened my mouth to talk to her

– I don't even know what I had planned to say. Console her? Deny everything? Play dumb? Spencer intervened.

'Don't even talk to her,' he said. 'Just go in there and pee into this cup.' He nodded at my parents' en suite bathroom.

My God, I'm fucked, I thought to myself. Game face, I told myself. You can get out of this. Just. Do. Not. Pee.

'I don't need to pee!' I protested. 'And I don't want a Dr Pepper.'

'I don't care,' came Spencer's response. 'You'll drink all of these until you do need to go.' As he said it he kicked what I now saw was a crate of Dr Pepper by his feet. He was serious. And much, much harder to negotiate with than either of my parents.

'We have been defending you all month. We have had your back. We have been calling everyone liars for years for you, and you've been lying to us the whole time.'

He had a point. But with my hazy addict's logic I had never seen it like that. The last thing I had wanted was to have caused a fuss. I stood there at the door to the bathroom, hesitating. He stood blocking the way back out of the bathroom.

'I don't care that you don't need to go. We'll wait.' He wasn't budging. I had never seen him so emotional. And worst of all, I started to realise that it wasn't just raw anger, he was hurt. And I was the one that had hurt him.

'I am not leaving until I hear that toilet flush and I have the sample,' he said, his voice breaking in pain.

I sat in there for an hour and a half, fighting it. But we all have our breaking points. Eventually, I peed. Oh, the dignity.

The minute I had handed over the sample that Spencer was so determined to obtain, I went into my bedroom and sat on the bed, wondering what would be next. How long did results take to come? What would they reveal? And how could I get away with carrying on as normal?

After a while my mom came in, her face still streaked with tears, and told me that Roxy's mom had called her the night before, having been kept up by my constant bathroom trips. She had no other evidence, but was sure that drug use was behind it. I didn't know what to say – I was reluctant to reveal too much in case – somehow – the tests came back in my favour. But I was also heartbroken by the sight of my mom so distressed. A short while later my dad came up to see me. He said simply that he was terribly worried about me. There had never been an upset like this in our family before, ever. So none of us really knew how to deal with it, what the procedure was.

'Steph,' said my dad, with a solemn face, 'you can go out tonight, because we love you and we want to trust you. But if we find out that you are doing anything, or if you do it ever again, we are going to sell your car.'

Somehow, this made me sadder than anything. I realised that my dad was still clinging to the hope that my drug use was just something I had done the night before. If he had had any inkling of the fact that this had been a way of life for me for over a year, the punishment would have been very different. He just didn't want me hurting – or his wife and son. Understanding this made me panic though, and my response was just one of anger.

'I HATE YOU! GET OUT OF MY ROOM NOW!' I blazed at him. He told me to calm down, and left.

I stayed up there crying, raging and ringing my friends, for hours. That night I went to bed without smoking meth for the first time in months, and was too scared to sleep. The paranoia set in and I was convinced that someone was going to come and take me away in the night, to one of those rehab boot camps that Californian parents so often threatened their kids with. The fear began to consume me, and I decided to barricade myself into my room. There wasn't a lock on the door but I took scarves and tried to bind the door handle closed. I lay there in the dark, my brain a fog of anxiety. But at no point did I think that not doing drugs might be the sensible route forward.

The next day my mom came back from the doctor's crying again. She had the test results from my urine sample. And she also had pages upon pages of printouts of information. But this time, there was no anger on either side. I had made it through the night without being whisked away to boot camp, and she had made it home without me running away. Instead of there being a tirade of recriminations and accusations, she simply sat at the kitchen table, spread the test results and leaflets in front of her and put her head in her hands.

'Stephanie, this is the question: how are you not dead?' Her voice was calm, but sad. And, I think, genuinely curious. I couldn't answer. 'The amount of methamphetamine you have inside of you is staggering. Do you even know what it is?'

I tried to explain what I thought it was. That it was like my prescribed Adderall, which I was still taking, but a bit more as I'd been feeling so sad.

But, for the first time, someone with actual facts was now explaining it to me. My mom had of course no experience of this kind of thing, but had, to her credit, gone out and got herself informed. The print-outs were covered with highlighting and underlining. She showed me information about meth's ingredients, how it was made, how it could be cut with all sorts of other terrifying substances. She produced endless photographs of people who had suffered from long-term meth addictions. She showed me what it would do to my teeth, diagrams of what it was doing to my internal organs, statistics about how long I could expect to survive if I carried on this way.

Literally all of this was news to me. It's one thing to have an instinct that perhaps you're not living a clean and healthy life. And it was only really the shady people around the drug that had given me those clues. After all, I had thought there were no negative side effects. I was young and healthy, I kept telling myself. But it's quite another thing to be faced with endless data and frightening imagery by someone you love, who is being calm and kind.

'Why are you doing this to yourself?' was all my mother asked, at the end of her explanation. 'Because you won't survive if you carry on.'

Finally, I accepted that my fun, drawback-free drug, that had been making me so happy since my adolescent depression kicked in, might not be as without consequence as I had hoped. I accepted that yes, meth might be as dirty and toxic as the people that it had made me mix with. And that it was only going to get worse. And yes, I accepted that I should probably stop. So that afternoon, following a long, heartfelt chat with my mom, I drove into town, circling around until I saw a massive dumpster behind a restaurant. I pulled up, got out, and threw my Hello Kitty bag full of meth and meth paraphernalia into it.

I had promised my mom that that would be the end of meth, and it would be. The things she had told me had frightened me out of wanting to do it ever again. And honestly, since that day, I haven't. The trouble was, no one had mentioned cocaine. Not Spencer, not my mom, not any of the doctors' notes and leaflets, and certainly not me.

Because by then, I had already started using it.

3

The same Nicole who had given me meth for the first time had also introduced me to cocaine a few months back, and I had been taking it from time to time, mostly at parties. It was far from a way of life, in the way that meth had become. But obviously it was not ideal. I was still a kid of seventeen, and I was regularly carrying around enough drugs to have gotten me a sizeable prison sentence.

Nicole was seriously bad news. She had now left high school and was working full time as a dealer, with her brothers. They shared a mansion in Brentwood, largely left to their own devices by their dad. Three kids, left alone in what had become a drug den under almost permanent stake out from the LAPD.

So Nicole's house had become party central, and when

I was not with my girl friends, I would hang out there. Nicole always had bricks of cocaine. And bricks is not a turn of phrase – she actually had blocks of solid cocaine the size of house bricks, which she would shave a little off when she fancied doing some. This may have been a turning point in losing any sense of perspective on the volume of drugs I was about to start taking. If the person you first see taking cocaine is shaving shards off a block that could be mistaken for a house brick, you are at risk of never knowing how much cocaine is a little cocaine, and how much is . . . a huge amount.

This was the spirit with which I entered rehab. Yes, the meth had to stop. But how could my tiny little slivers of coke be a problem at all? Best not to mention it to anyone, get through a month or so of whatever rehab my parents had lined up, and then carry on with a little party coke when I needed it, I mean felt like it . . .

Once I had got rid of my meth and its paraphernalia, I had to get the coke out of the house, so I took the lot (and I can now see that it was a lot) over to my friend Claire's house.

'Could you look after this for me for a while?' I asked, casually. 'I've got to do this rehab for a bit and I probably shouldn't have it around until my mom's off my back.'

It was as if I was getting the chocolate out of the kitchen cupboard for a bit while I was on a diet. But Claire said she was happy to keep it, and as some of the other girls were now starting to take it at parties it didn't seem too alarming to her.

The plan my parents had for my recovery was a three-pronged one. They had taken a lot of advice, and were even going to Al-Anon for relatives of addicts themselves. But in hindsight, they were not fully informed about the extent of my problem, and none of us knew how much further I had yet to go until I was ready to let drugs go. So everything they had planned at this point was doomed to failure whether it was a good idea or not. And some of it really wasn't a good idea.

I went back to having therapy which was fine, but it wasn't really very targeted and I was still not terribly inclined to open up about things, especially now that I had this secret life of drugs contacts. The therapist diagnosed me with borderline personality disorder, which really did not sit well with me because the Winona Ryder character in the movie *Girl, Interrupted* had borderline personality disorder and I thought that just wasn't me. I was so disheartened, sad for weeks thinking about it, but I guess that was the me they saw when I was freshly off the meth, and that was all they had to work with. Still, they put me on some new medication for my depression, so I figured it couldn't be all bad.

I was also attending the Of One Mind clinic every day, which was fine too, although it was more of a monitoring thing. I would have to show up after school and pee in a cup. It was sort of like an after-school club for the naughtiest kids in high school. The theory was that if I was reliable enough to keep showing up and passing the drugs tests, I would be getting clean anyway. And that was fine – I really didn't find it too hard to stop with the meth, as my attitude was that it was just for a while until I could get on with business as usual.

The third prong, and perhaps the weirdest part of the rehab, was the drugs therapist that I was sent to. Bob Timmins was counsellor to the stars, with a practice on Main Street, Venice. I can see what my parents were thinking, as he was an iconic figure, but I'm not sure he was the right guy for me . . .

Bob Timmins had been an addict himself, and had clearly lived one hell of a life. He's dead now, but then he looked kind of like a roadie, or even a *Sons of Anarchy*-style gang member. Either way, he had had a pretty moody past before he got sober himself, and he wasn't afraid to show that in how he presented himself. He had been in prison for armed robbery and then lived on the streets before he cleaned up in his twenties. He had long dark hair, a dark beard and was covered in tattoos. He wore a lot of leather, and silver jewellery, and had clearly been developing his rocker look since it was invented.

But he wasn't what the passer-by on the street might have assumed he was. In fact, he was a hugely respected figure in the music industry, who had helped to get acts like Aerosmith and Mötley Crüe clean. And you don't have to know too much about the history of music to know that those guys were really, really into drugs. He was known as the guy who could help even the most lost of lost causes out, and he had even got the music industry to implement new working practices such as having a 'clean' room at big events, shows and music studios, for artists who were in recovery.

Consequently, I had no doubt that he was a great guy with the very best of intentions. And that he had probably helped people whose friends and family had long given up on them. But he didn't seem to be able to find a way to identify with me on any level. He had developed a specialist area, and it wasn't relevant to me. Instead of trying to get to the bottom of why I was taking drugs, or why I was developing what could probably by now be described as addictive patterns, he preferred instead to chat more vaguely and generally.

A typical session would begin with him asking me how things were. As far as I was concerned he was just a guy being polite, and I didn't really want to cause any trouble, so I would just say I was fine, that everything was going really well thanks very much. Then, instead of maybe leading the questioning or directing my attention to areas of my behaviour that were inappropriate or unhealthy, he would just fill the uncomfortable silence with . . . rock anecdotes.

I'm not kidding, and I know it sounds crazy, but he would literally just tell me stories about life on the road with bands over the last fifteen years. He wasn't bragging about his celebrity connections, and I am sure that he absolutely had his clients' best interests at heart. I think he was often telling me these long-winded rock anecdotes as a cautionary tale, as at the end he would always stress that there were only three ways out of addiction: 'You get clean, you go to jail or you die.' But instead he kind of glorified it to me. I don't think he meant to, but I was an impressionable teenager, and telling me stories about how the biggest rock stars in the world had all done drugs didn't really put me off.

When he would open a session with, 'Stephanie, is there anything you want to talk about today, anything you're struggling with?' I would feel unable to engage. I had been going to various therapists for about four years solidly now, and no one had really put their finger on why I felt the way I did. I was done talking, and was also the same old people-pleaser I'd always been. So instead of replying with any queries or worries of my own, my reply would be a gentle, 'Oh no, I'm fine, don't worry about me.' I wouldn't offer to talk – I was all talked out. So before long there would come his usual anecdote-opener: 'Well, this one time with Nikki Sixx . . .' I wasn't a rock star. My problems were not the result of hard living on a tour bus. I was in the wrong place.

It also seemed like a massive betrayal of his previous clients' confidentiality that he would tell me these things, however well-meaning he was in telling me them. It didn't incline me to open up to him at all. His stories of prison all seemed so far-fetched. He even told me he had been raped in there, which didn't make for a very comfortable counselling session that week. He would constantly warn me about what a dark place it was, and how I never wanted to end up there – but that it was inevitable if drugs stayed in my life. It seemed ridiculous to me that that could possibly be my fate. How on earth could I end up in jail? Little did I know that it would only be a couple of years before I did, twice . . .

After a couple of months, it seemed to the concerned outsiders in my life that I was 'better'. I did feel much better – of course I did, I had stopped taking meth all day! But the inner core of sadness and anxiety that I wasn't perfect or even normal remained. And for as long as it did, I suppose there was going to be a part of me that was still going to want to numb those sensations.

I was now a senior in high school, and in a crowd of older guys who had been seniors when I was a freshman and girls I had known from growing up in the Palisades. They were even older than my brother and we were going out drinking and to clubs in central LA on the weekends. I still wanted to smoke weed from time to time at a friend's house, or do some coke on a big night out every few months. Socially, I was very much back in the game. The trouble was, my mom was still threatening to give me random drug tests – and occasionally she saw those threats through. I had to find a way around this, and I did.

Every few days I would ask my friend Jen to go to the bathroom and pee in a cup for me. When she returned, I would pour that 'clean' pee into a clear plastic ziplock bag, the sort that you might put some kitchen leftovers into. What kind of a friend is constantly prepared to do that for you, you might ask. Well, that was the culture at school by then. A lot of us were doing recreational drugs on the evenings and weekends, and we were prepared to help each other out.

Once I had my fresh pouch of pee, I would put the bag down the front of my Ugg boot. This way, the pee would settle (in its bag) around the front of my foot, out of sight to anyone who wasn't looking directly down on the boot from above. It meant that I always had a clean drug sample on me, and I was able to carry on with whatever recreational drugs I still felt like doing. I was constantly prepared, ready to head straight to the bathroom if my mom jumped at me with a cup and told me she needed a sample before I had a chance to go upstairs to my bedroom.

As plans go, it was pretty ingenious. But I cannot lie. If you are walking upstairs from a long day in the classroom and as you lift your leg to climb the stairs to the bedroom you see a bag of piss curling around your foot, it doesn't feel great. I told myself that it was evidence of my own ingenuity, but in truth, it was not ideal. Realistically, only people who are suffering from some sort of health crisis should be carrying bags of bodily fluids around with them. I suppose, in hindsight, that was exactly what was happening to me.

Continuing to keep these secrets from my mom made me quite paranoid about what might happen next, especially as, compared with my previous meth days, I really was taking drugs very rarely. I was wise enough to know that she wouldn't see it that way though. What might she discover? What might show up in tests? How might she respond to any results that didn't come up clear? I was about to leave high school by now, and was desperate for freedom from what I (very unfairly) saw as her constant surveillance. Of course she just wanted to do whatever she could to keep me clean and healthy – both of my parents did. But I couldn't see that then, so I opted for college as far away as I could manage. Paris.

4

I had been obsessed by Paris for years, and had long dreamed of just getting there for a holiday. I eventually did visit the summer before my senior year of high school, and it was everything I had imagined and hoped it would be. I was there for Bastille Day, and spent it sitting under the Eiffel Tower with a picnic blanket, sipping wine and watching the fireworks setting the sky alight. Then, in spring 2004 the show *Sex and the City* aired the episodes when Carrie goes to Paris and my obsession grew stronger. I had to get there!

So when one of my tutors (I had them round the clock by this point, to keep me up to date with lessons and homework in spite of my every attempt to keep socialising whenever I could) told me that she had gone to the American University in Paris, I leapt at the opportunity. I

researched all of the possible courses I could do, applied
and got myself a place to study anthropology and compara-
tive literature. Next I looked up the sort of areas I might
like to live in. I found an apartment on Rue de Vaugirard
and set myself up to leave the country. There was still the
small matter of convincing my parents though.

The fact that I had got myself together enough to organise
all of this was testament to the fact that if occupied and
happy, I could keep my mind clear and get on with positive
things when I wanted to. My parents were worried for me
– they weren't convinced that I needed to be so far away
to be happy – but they saw my commitment to the idea
and decided to trust me. I had proved myself with the drug
tests, and after all, I was going to study not to party. My
campaigning worked: at the end of that summer I had a
cute going-away party with adorable little Parisian invitations. And not long after that, I was there.

My parents came with me to settle me in and help me
furnish my apartment. We even bought early video phones
and called each other on them every day once they went
back to LA. The positive terms that we left on and my enthu-
siasm to study meant that when they left Paris and I started
my new European life, my confidence was higher than it had
been for years. Once they were gone I missed them hugely,
but I was ready for the challenge. And it was a great help
that Paris was everything I'd dreamed it would be. From the
elegant grey buildings to the exquisite fashions, everything

looked just like the movie dream that I had been hoping for. And to top it off, the Parisians really did walk around all day with tiny dogs under their arms or in their handbags, taking them to bars and cafés whenever they wanted!

In my first week I arrived at class and looked around the room thinking, 'Hmmm, who am I going to find to talk to here?' It was a time before you could just stand in the corner and fiddle with your mobile phone if you felt new, nervous or awkward – you had to get stuck in. I had always gotten along with people at high school even at my lowest ebb, so I walked up to the girl who looked like she could be fun and just hoped that she could understand my wobbly French.

She had long dark hair, a great smile and a black leather Chanel jacket on. The only way to find out is to ask, so I just walked up and grinned at her.

'Do you want to take figure drawing with me?'

'Okay,' she replied, in English.

'Hang on, you're American?' I said.

'Sure am. But I live here,' she said. 'My mom has been married to a Frenchman for years.'

And with that my Parisian social group began. After classes Alana asked if I wanted to hang out, and of course I did. I discovered that she had lived in the city since she was eight, and her step-dad was in fact some sort of French aristocrat. That first afternoon we headed to meet a friend of hers on a bridge across the Seine, as we were all going to hang out for the afternoon with a third friend in Neuilly.

I'll never forget walking towards that bridge and seeing one of the coolest looking girls I've ever laid eyes on waiting for us. She was Algerian, and had a totally funky street-fashion vibe going on. She had massive hair in a big pony, and one huge hoop earring, she was wearing a flashy top, rolled-up boyfriend-length jeans and an enormous pair of high heels. She looked incredible, as if she were filming for a music video, not just waiting to hang out with some friends. But that's how things were in Paris, everyone took great care over their look, and they weren't afraid to show it. In LA everyone is expected to look perfect all of the time too . . . but God forbid you should look as if you tried, rather than just having walked off the beach looking like that!

From there we caught the train to Neuilly, a super-swanky residential suburb, where we headed to Alana's friend Jean-Luc's place. Jean-Luc was the most devastatingly handsome, immaculately styled gay guy. Honestly he looked like an aftershave advertisement come to life, and his apartment was just as deluxe. As I looked around at the group that afternoon, while they were telling me about all the plans they were making for the next few months, and all the fun they would be having with me, I couldn't believe my luck. As if to seal the new friendship, Jean-Luc offered me some weed. We had a great afternoon chatting in a combination of English, French and 'Franglais', which is what we called our mashed-up attempts to speak a bit of both, depending on which words we knew. That evening

I wobbled back home to my Montparnasse apartment as high as a kite.

Apart from the occasional joint with Jean-Luc, I was largely drug-free in Paris, and entirely happy about it. The only *real* substance abuse going on while I was there was with carbohydrates. I was eating bread and croissants every day, pizza whenever I felt like it and almost non-stop cheeses. I learned to love duck, and escargots and of course champagne. Lots of champagne! As far as I was concerned, it was a waste of time being in Paris if I wasn't going to indulge in everything the city had on offer, so I really let myself go for it.

I knew I wanted to get a dog from the minute I set off for France. We'd always had pets at home, and my dad and I were especially devoted dog lovers. But my parents begged me not to, they didn't want me to be tied down, bound to nights in alone when I was in a new city trying to make friends and experience everything Paris had to offer. I took their advice at first, and resisted the temptation to run to the nearest pet store and live the dream. But as luck would have it, within the very first month Paris blessed me with a dog that I still love to this day.

After a few weeks of college I was walking with Alana down one of the Montparnasse streets not far from where I was living, when I heard whimpering under a parked car. It was dusk on a grey drizzly day – the sort of weather that Europeans always complain about and Californians love. The street was cobbled and I was in heels, so it was a bit of a totter about before I could work out which car the noise was coming from.

I leaned over and spotted what I thought at first was a large sewer rat beneath the car. It was tiny, soaking wet and almost entirely hairless. And it looked even balder in the rain which was now coming down. The only thing that reassured me it wasn't a rat was the fact that it didn't scuttle away from me, but let me reach down and try to pull it out.

Alana and I realised immediately that the animal was very sick, and needed help. She knew where there was an animal hospital, so off we went.

'We're not sure that we can save her, she just doesn't seem to have eaten for days – possibly longer.'

The news was bad, and even worse for me having to wait and have it translated by Alana as we tried to work out whether the dog could be saved. We begged them to do whatever they could, and the tiny creature ended up spending three nights in there before they told me she would survive – and was well enough to come home with me.

She had had no collar and no chip, so she was all mine. As she dried off, we realised she was a 'Yorkie', a Yorkshire Terrier. I named her Kiki, and armed with some food and some drops for her, I took her back to the apartment to finish her convalescence. I absolutely adored that dog, and immediately became a full-time mom to her. For those first few weeks I would take the bus back to the apartment between classes to give her medicine and drops. It made me so happy to drop by and see her perk up at the sight of my face! (And, no doubt the medicine bottle.) I thrived on the sense of responsibility it gave me and the more I achieved, the more I felt I could achieve. Best of all, instead of her holding me back like my parents had feared a dog would, she helped me to fit right in!

Once Kiki was fully well, she started to accompany me everywhere – I was living the Parisian dream! She had a huge wardrobe of outfits that I would buy all over the city, but mostly in Le Bon Marché. They took up half my room, and my living room was always covered in her toys. She became part of the gang, coming to most of my classes (the teaching staff were always very indulgent!), sitting on my lap in restaurants and following me on walks around the beautiful city. These days, she lives with my parents in LA, and my mom sends me pictures of her the whole time. I think my parents love Kiki more than they love us. She's become the heart of the family. I mean she's all my mom talks about. Still! I am so happy that she's so loved.

All in all, Paris and my time there was exactly as I had imagined it. I had Kiki, I had a group of creative and imaginative friends, and I was really enjoying my studies. Who would have thought that I would develop such a love of Freud? Or become such an enthusiastic participant in figure-drawing classes? Well, actually, enjoying figure drawing isn't that hard to imagine – given that it was literally drawing naked guys. I had no idea that that was what it would actually be!

Alana and I had the best time in those classes, always pulling faces and giggling. Everyone else there was terribly serious, and it's not as if we didn't want to learn – but honestly, the mystery of who would be stripping in front of us each week was sometimes too much not to giggle at! We'd be there standing by our easels with our pencils at the ready, when in would walk a guy in a robe. Sometimes it was a wrinkly old man, and sometimes it was a super-hot guy. We would never know, and we'd never quite know which would make us giggle more. It could be that someone was posing like a Greek god when they really didn't look like one. Or it could be that it was someone so hot we were barely able to stand. But either way it was one of the highlights of the week. After a while we all became convinced that the teacher was hooking up with the models, as we had way fewer women than guys. It was France, after all . . .

I planned to spend all four years of my course there, but in the end didn't even complete one. Over Christmas I went back to LA for the holidays and was told I would not be going back. I was stunned. It seems that in my absence, and following a visit from Spencer who seemed not to have taken to my French friends, my family had become convinced I was back taking drugs. I have never really worked out why, and it is very painful for me to think about. I can only imagine that because I had proved untrustworthy in the past, they felt too anxious about having me in a different country, not able to make sure I was clean and having regular drug tests.

I had left Europe with only one bag, my purse, and Kiki (who by now had a little doggie passport, and sat on my lap on the Air France flight like a true Parisian). And now I was told I wasn't allowed to go back. The hugest of arguments followed, but my parents were unpersuadable.

'Fine,' I eventually said. 'I'll go back and pack up all my stuff.' I had no intention of ever returning if I could just get back to Paris. But I guess they knew that. I was told they were sending my sister Kristin and her new husband, who she had married while I was away, to pack up my apartment for me. There was to be no more discussion about it.

I was devastated. Beyond devastated. Not just that I was not allowed back to Paris, but that I had made enough mistakes in my past that they would continue to have an impact on my future. The irony of me being clean in Paris, having a great friendship group and getting on with my studies and that being what made my parents want me home was too much to bear.

But instead of doing anything constructive with my anger, I let it consume me.

'You know what? If you think I'm on drugs, I may as well be,' I thought. So I picked up the phone, and then went straight round to my old 'friend' Nicole's house. She had an apartment in Brentwood by now and was delighted to see me. She'd been to rehab too, and I guess it had worked as well as mine had.

'Hook me up with whatever you've got,' I told her. And she was more than happy to help.

That was the day I started doing OxyContin. She told me I'd like it, and I took her at her word. As ever, I did little to no research into what it might actually be, but I'd heard people talking about it, and it came in a medicinal-looking pack, so that was enough for me. I was so unhappy then that I don't think I would have cared if I had known how toxic or addictive it could be. It is, after all, basically medical heroin, prescribed as a painkiller.

I basically moved into Nicole's apartment, so desperate was I not to be at home with my parents. I was no longer speaking to anyone in my entire family. I was still in shock that I would not be going back to Paris and my approach was nothing beyond fuck you guys. Their whole Paris judgement call had turned out to be a major backfire.

I was the angriest person in the world. The rage inside me was so strong that I felt it was going to overwhelm me if I didn't try to numb it, so this was the point at which I simply started subconsciously trying to kill myself with drugs. I was taking amounts upon amounts. Experimenting with pills, powders, whatever. And washing it all down with gallons of booze.

Any act of rebellion I could think of, I would do. Nicole and I were going out and partying, then getting up to ridiculous things like getting our tongues pierced. After a while, I stopped even bothering with the partying bit, just staying in to devote as much time as possible to drugs. I was taking whatever I could until I either threw up or passed out, pretty much every day. This was a world away from recreational cocaine; this was intense misery en route to becoming serious addiction. Again.

By March, things reached crisis point for Nicole and she decided to head back to rehab, at which point my parents intervened and set me up in a nearby apartment of my own. It was a two bedroomed place in Brentwood, really close to them. Our relationship was improving, but the damage done by those intense weeks of bingeing on drugs was deeper than I realised. Paris had shown that they still didn't trust me, and I had now effectively proved all of their anxieties valid. But I had little trust in them too, seeing my recent return to drug taking as their fault.

I knew that was wrong though, and I knew it was me and only me who had taken those drugs. But I couldn't overcome the anger and rage, and this was only compounded by the fact I had so little else going on in my life now. My studies had been cut short, yet I had no job. There was no social media back in 2005, so my Parisian friends were all rather out of sight, out of mind. The time difference meant we could rarely talk, so we rarely did, and so we drifted out of touch.

There was no direction in my life, nothing to aim for, and nothing to look forward to. Everyone else seemed to be getting on with their own thing, while no one at all seemed to need or want me for anything. My friends were all travelling, married or in college. Most of them were in New York at NYU. Kristin was focussed on starting her own family and Spencer was laying down the tracks for his own career, even if to me it just seemed like him being left alone to mess around with his best friend Brody, pretending to get some TV show made. I was left wading through a world of depression, with no clear way out, ever.

When I look back on this time, I can see that I was doing what I always did when the depression started to nip: comparing myself to other people instead of focussing on what I *could* do. This mentality was always the root of my problems, but it took me so damn long to learn that or to develop skills not to do it as much. That's how I stay happy now – by not letting myself go down that path of comparison. Eleven years ago . . . not so much. On my nineteenth birthday I reached my lowest ebb. Slowly, it dawned on me that there was only really one way out.

'Okay, enough,' I thought. 'It's time to end it.'

That day was particularly bad, for all sorts of reasons. Nineteen seemed too old to be so directionless. I had a dreadful hangover, and what I now know was a serious depressive episode was engulfing me. I fell out with my mom, who had been nagging at me again to get a job. I hated having her telling me what to do with my life; she wanted me to start working, no matter what, and I didn't see why I should be waiting tables while Spencer was goofing around in front of cameras 'for a living'.

As far as I could see things, through my anxious, depressed haze, Spencer was perfect in my parents' eyes. He didn't have to get a sensible job because he hadn't messed up by being imperfect like me. It seemed so unfair. Why should I be punished for being depressed, and he rewarded for being a happier person anyway? They saw him as reliable, likeable, a go-getter. And all I could see was my annoying brother getting away with what looked like goofing around and making it a career while I was still finding the simplest of things a struggle.

Drugs and alcohol are depressants. So a depressed person taking them is not going to have the clearest of minds. But that day I felt I had perfect clarity and only one option. Suicide.

This was not a cry for help. I sincerely believed that it was the most sensible option. A couple of times in the past, when I had stayed up all night smoking meth alone and had reached the intense anxiety of the early morning, I had felt close to wanting to end things. But those moments of darkness had always been fleeting, and had passed without me dwelling on them. This time, I was only growing stronger in my conviction, my mind becoming darker and more clouded. I felt I hated my family and that I was hated by them.

I got into bed and surrounded myself with everything I

needed. I took OxyContin, and some 'xanbars' which are extra-long tablets of the powerful anti-anxiety medication Xanax, which are designed to be broken up into smaller sections for taking tiny amounts. I did some coke, and chased it all down with whiskey. I lay there in my sweat-pants, watching the TV become hazy and waiting for oblivion. I didn't know when that would come, so I just kept going. I smoked a joint, did some more of everything, tried to find a point where numbness would embrace me.

Mercifully, my belief that my family didn't care about me was as wrong as so many of my choices that day. My mother, who had clearly realised how distressed I was when we spoke, had decided to come round and see me in person. She knew I was in – she could see lights on, and my car – but by the time she arrived I was no longer able to answer the door. Eventually – amazingly – she found an open window and managed to get into the building and find me. To my eternal gratitude, she was able to call for help in time.

I woke up, and I was in UCLA Medical Center. My first instinct was relief that I was still alive. But it was followed by huge regret that I was still there, to cause trouble for my family. I didn't want to be in hospital, but once you've tried to overdose, these things are removed from being your choice. I was in ER for a short while, before being moved to the A South ward, which was for people with mental-health problems. I was sleeping in a hospital bed, diagnosed as someone with mental-health issues rather than someone with an addiction. Not for the first time, those looking after me seemed to be seeing my depression as separate from my relationship with drugs, rather than a hideously entwined situation. At no point had any medical professional really seemed to understand how complex my problem was. None of the kind faces had looked at me and said anything that had remotely made me think, 'Yes! That is how I feel, this is the problem! Now how do I deal with this?' It just seemed like a wall was between us still.

Of course, I was glad to be receiving some sort of help, and as the month that I was there passed, I felt greater relief that my mother had gotten to me in time. But my memories of this stay in hospital are of crippling sadness. My family all came to visit me, and I just felt tremendous guilt. Once again, I was dragging the family down.

With hindsight, I can see that they didn't feel this – they were all just worried about me. They constantly showed me love and support, bringing me get well cards, flowers and gifts. One time my brother, who I had convinced myself was so busy being perfect, came to visit me bringing the gift of a beautiful gold ring. No one blamed me, no harsh words were said, no one tried to make me feel worse. 'How did it get to this?' seemed to be the main emotion that we were all feeling.

After a month I was released from hospital, and in time my parents and I agreed that I would start studying at FIDM, the Fashion Institute of Design and Merchandising in Los Angeles. I was fragile, and still living between my parents' house and my own apartment but I was happy to have a fresh direction, and for a little while it seemed as if things had steadied out again. Life was calmer, I started to get busier, and perhaps things could have stayed that way. I doubt it though. Because despite being more content than I had been for a while, I was still doing the odd bit of coke at parties, and taking OxyContin from time to time. I wasn't thin, or wired, just spaced out and relaxed. I was no trouble to anyone, and nowhere near my previous suicidal state. But, in short, I was an addict who was still using drugs recreationally: aka a disaster waiting to happen. Drug addiction had become a part of me. It was as familiar as a body part. Just there, never going away, always needing to be fed.

And then I met Amber.

Amber was an old friend from high school who I hadn't seen since before Paris. I didn't know it then, but the reason I hadn't seen her was because she had been in a very bad car accident, as a result of her being DUI (Driving Under the Influence), and had gone to jail for it. I literally bumped into her at the gas station when I had popped out to buy cigarettes one evening. It seemed like she was doing the same. We were both in sweatpants with our hair scraped back; the only difference was that she was now covered in tattoos.

'Oh my God, how have you been?' I asked, thrilled to see someone who might not know what I had been up to lately.

'I've just got back into town,' she replied, clearly being equally discreet about her own recent past.

'Look at us,' I said. 'So lonely! Neither of us have any friends any more! Why don't you come over? I'm cooking.'

Twenty minutes later we were both on my sofa, looking down at my coffee table.

'So do you still use drugs?' she had asked me.

'A little bit,' I'd replied. 'Mainly just pills and stuff though.'

I was reluctant to let on how deep my problems had gone. Then she showed me what she had. A huge assortment of pills, weed and other bits. Which were now spread out on my coffee table. The inevitable happened.

'Wow, this is great,' I thought. And for a while it was.

That night we got really fucked up and made a stir-fry together. Again, I felt the relief of being able to do mundane things but do them one step removed from reality. And from that day on we were inseparable.

I had convinced myself that taking prescription drugs was much better and far less of a problem than taking street drugs. It was medication. These were legal substances. This in turn meant that my mom couldn't get me on it as I always had an answer for her. 'I need them, they are my medication.' I had come full circle, to the day I first took meth believing it was no different to Adderall.

But if taking those pills had been a necessity, I wouldn't have been taking them like I did – planning my activities around them and using them as a crutch for my entertainment and happiness. I was doing more than merely medicating myself. I was taking huge amounts of OxyContin and Xanax then going to Barneys to go shopping while feeling blurry and doped up. Then I was spending days taking excess Adderall and some coke in order to feel high. It was a chemical merry-go-round, doing whatever it took to keep my brain switched off and my feelings numbed.

It was the spring that the TV show *Lost* was closing its incredible first season, and Amber and I were both instantly obsessed by it – everyone was. There were huge billboards all over LA and there had been for months. The weird creepiness of the storylines and the gorgeous desert island setting were the perfect combination for creating moreish viewing. And, as luck would have it, Amber's dad was a director and executive producer on the show.

As we slumped on the sofa one evening, Amber had an idea.

'Why don't we go to Hawaii and help my dad with the show?' she said.

'Are you kidding?'

'Oh come on, all we do is get high and go shopping. We should get out there.'

'YES!' I replied. 'It's a great idea!'

It really wasn't.

5

It all seemed so simple at first. I took a semester off my studies at FIDM, and Amber and I moved to Hawaii together. This time – as opposed to Paris – my parents were okay with things. There were two main reasons. The first was that I would be under the wing of Amber's dad. We were staying in a condo in the same complex as him, and our jobs were indirectly working for him. And then of course there was the fact that I would be working. It was my first proper job, and a chance to get away from Los Angeles and the negativity that had been dogging me there. I knew Hawaii, as it is where we had gone on family holidays for years, so there wasn't even the anxiety of going somewhere unfamiliar. Amber's dad had set us up with an incredible condo, and we had jobs all lined up for us – Amber was going to be in wardrobe, exactly as she'd wanted, and I was going to be largely on set. Given that the sets were all basically the beach or the jungle, it was non-stop outdoors fun. I had my little walkie-talkie, making me feel like a proper industry insider. I was in charge of getting the actors when they were needed on set, so off I'd go in my little golf buggy, as happy as I'd been in years.

When we arrived on Hawaii *Lost* frenzy was approaching its peak. Everyone was on tenterhooks for the second season: the show's weird combination of action, science fiction and fantasy had caught the world's imagination. The whole world was talking about it – whether it was the intense plot surrounding the mysteriously crashed plane, the strange goings-on on the island the survivors had landed on . . . or just how incredibly hot the cast were. And we were the first to be a part of it all as the next season unfolded.

I was happy and busy all day on set, then in the evenings I would call my family and give them snippets of insider information about what we'd been doing. We were getting close again; in a weird way the distance helped. My whole family finally seemed to have a bit of admiration for me – that I had at last got myself together, got a great job and was actually making a go of it. And I really was! We weren't paid that much, but I was working hard – six days a week, and long hours each day – and seemed to be getting along with all the cast and crew.

It was those long hours that were the seed of my next

crop of problems, though. I was completely unused to being in any sort of routine, let alone one that required me to be up and out of the house at quite extreme times of day. So I did what I thought any responsible working adult would do, and started to medicate myself a little – just to get the best out of the situation. It was my old friend Adderall that I turned to first, to give me that pep that was needed on those early mornings on set. I had long discovered that taking the correct amount might have made me feel low but that taking significantly more did quite the opposite, giving me the fuel to keep going. It seemed entirely reasonable, committed even. The pills weren't that hard to get hold of as there were other members of the crew using them, so it seemed pretty normal.

As the work hours increased and my body adapted to the drugs, I started taking a little more. Until all day I was fuelled by Adderall Adderall Adderall. Then after a while I needed some Xanax to get to sleep as the Adderall was still coursing through my veins at 1.00 am when we'd finish on set. Still, it seemed to be the responsible way to get the work done. I wasn't drinking or partying at all. This was a question of keeping up with something I was totally unused to, in an environment where no one was saying no when I asked for the 'medication'.

Our one day off was a Sunday, when Amber and I would go to the Neiman Marcus in Honolulu and spend our pay cheques. After a few weeks we had got to know everyone in the store. We would walk in and the staff would smile, get us glasses of champagne and say, 'Hey girls! How was the week on set?' We started to think of them as our friends, they always seemed so pleased to see us, and we always had such a good time there. We were known as 'the LA girls' and we'd delight them with our mix of showbiz gossip and bulging wallets. They had a couple of great customers, providing lots of on-set news, and lots of healthy commission.

It was a perfect few months, and to my delight I even found someone who could supply me with OxyContin for when I really needed to relax. Yeah, OxyContin again. It's a painkiller, but basically it's chemical heroin. Like I said, because I was surrounded by other people doing the same thing, this behaviour seemed entirely normal. Combined with the fact that, just like at school, I wasn't falling behind at work and I was still maintaining good relationships with everyone, there seemed to be no problem at all. I was a functioning addict. And besides there was no more dirty meth, no more skanky dealers, no scabs on my skin, and no negative consequences. Yet.

This idea that everything was going brilliantly was compounded even further when we were invited to come back and work on the third season. We had been formally offered the jobs, our parents had okayed the plan for us to come back when shooting began again, and we were going to head back to LA for a bit before returning for the next batch of filming. I was so excited. This was my life now, working in the industry in an incredible location . . . with a plentiful supply of 'meds'.

But of course, I was a full-blown addict again now. My every waking moment was dictated by pills, and my sleep was brought on by them as well. It didn't matter that they came in nice clean pharmaceutical bottles these days, the routine was the same – get up, take drugs; feel happy, take drugs; feel sad, take drugs; feel bored, take drugs; want to party, take drugs; want to sleep, take drugs. The carousel just wasn't stopping. And, like all addicts, it didn't take too long before I was chasing the next high. This time, I wanted actual morphine.

I had heard people talking on set, and realised that there were things called 'morphine pops' that were used in hospitals for those in the military who have just lost a limb, people who have terminal cancer, and other cases where absolutely nothing else will do. You suck on the 'candy' which releases the morphine directly, and quickly, into your body through the thin membranes in your mouth. The fastest, most effective way to get one of the most powerful opiates in the world into your system. Perfect.

I was so excited when I found out that there was someone who could get some. I looked forward to it for ages, and planned when I was going to do them. Because my drug intake was now so big, I had left the days of just taking a bit of Adderall or Xanax to 'level out' far behind me. I was now taking the pills recreationally, to block out whatever my 'normal' moods might have been. In short, I did them in order to make doing other stuff more interesting. Being myself was no longer enough – being myself, but high, was the usual goal.

The plan was to combine my two favourite Hawaii activities in one glorious end-of-season-two double-trip: we'd take the morphine pops, and head to Neiman Marcus for one final shopping spree. After all, we figured, we needed a new wardrobe for the new season. It was a gorgeous sunny day, and we were in the car in the parking lot on top of Neiman Marcus. We took a bunch of pills with some water, sat with the sun on our faces, and decided to start on the morphine pops. So relaxing.

But all of a sudden we were both throwing up out of the side of the car.

'Nooooooo!' I was shrieking! Most of us would be freaked out if we suddenly started throwing up in the middle of the day because of all the pills we had taken. But that's not why I was shrieking. I, well, I was just worried that I'd wasted the pills and I'd have to take them all again. My health? That was the very last thing on my mind.

So half an hour later, once we'd had some water, fixed our hair and straightened ourselves up again, we took a load more pills. The whole thing started again. Only this time, a little slower. We shared a joint to keep us calm, then started on the morphine pops.

'Stay cool, and take it from here,' we told ourselves, as we swayed out of the car in the early afternoon heat. We were already in a haze of oblivion, moving slowly towards the store. We were both in long flowing dresses, the sort of boho chic that everyone was in that summer. We were wearing Pucci headscarves and huge sunglasses. Very *Valley of the Dolls* chic.

'No one will suspect a thing,' I said to Amber.

'Of course not, babe,' she replied. 'And anyway, they're our friends!'

We headed into the store and the same routine as usual began.

'Hi girls!' came the voices, as we passed the make-up counters on the entrance.

'So great to see you!' they said, as we headed up to womenswear.

'We have a little something for you!' said another voice, as we entered the dressing rooms. And a bottle of champagne appeared.

Amber and I spent some time wandering around the store picking out clothes we *needed* to try on. The heap got bigger and bigger, and soon we were sitting on the floor of a huge dressing room, piles of designer goods tottering around us. We swigged on the champagne. We took a few more pills as we were feeling so great we didn't want this, the Greatest Shopping Trip of All Time, to lose its sparkle at any point. Oh I was sure no one heard my handbag rattling like maracas as the bottles of pills clanked around in it. In fact, where was everyone? It was so quiet in the store today . . .

As we sifted through the mountains of necessary purchases our mood began to shift. We seemed to have about $20,000 of clothes in there. But we 'only' had about $5,000 worth of spending money. Shit, we couldn't get all this. That wasn't fair!

'Basically, baby, they owe us these clothes,' I announced to Amber, with the slurred confidence only someone in my state could achieve.

'You are soooright,' she replied.

'We are soooooogooodtothem!'

'We're keeping thizplace afloat.'

'And thisssssiss too good to leave behind. You need it.' I draped a headscarf over Amber.

'They-our friendzzzz. We they friendzzz.'

'Youknowit baby. We are so *loyal* to them. We only get onedayofff, and we come here. They need us.'

And so it continued. Before long, we had managed to convince ourselves that because of our months of solid-gold friendship with these guys, we really were within our rights to take all the goods we wanted. I should add at this point that I have no idea what these goods actually were. It was not a case of a couture dress that one of us had been longing for the entire season, or some jewellery that the other desperately wanted to wear for a very special occasion.

We were simply out of our minds on opiates and could see no logical reason why we would not be allowed to do exactly as we wanted. And what we wanted was a bunch of Marc Jacobs dresses, some Marni jewellery, probably a few Pucci bathing suits and some other random Hawaii glamour wear.

I have no memory of any of the staff being around while we were having these little chats. But something tells me they might have been keeping an eye on us. That's just hindsight talking, though, because this was the point at which we hatched our master plan. We knew we had to steal stuff, and there was only one way to do it undetected. We'd have to wear it.

Layering was in that summer. But I can't pretend that how we looked could possibly have been mistaken for any kind of a style statement. We didn't want to make things 'too obvious', so we set aside $4,000 worth of goods that we would buy. And simply started putting the rest on. I am not kidding when I say that the easiest way to describe what we must have looked like was Joey from *Friends* when he decides to wear all of his clothes at once. We got to the point where we couldn't physically get any more on to our bodies. Then, and only then, did we surrender to the fact that we'd gotten as much as we could. After all, we had to play it cool . . . or else someone might notice something.

We headed for the till, playing it cool. Ice cool. Still, the store remained strangely silent. There was almost no one talking as we walked past; I remember thinking how pretty the tinkling music on the sound system was. As the woman on the till started to ring up our purchases, I looked up out of the skylight and noticed that the sky was now entirely dark. It was night. We must have been in that dressing room for at least five hours, playing our endless game of 'Noooo darling, you take that one'.

Not that that's what I thought then. If anything, 'Oooh night is so pretty,' was all that crossed my mind at that point.

Before too long our purchases were bagged up and paid for. But still, the eerie silence. 'Is it the drugs?' I wondered. It wasn't, it was that the store was closing. That, and the fact that everyone was staring at us. 'Byeee!' we waved, laughing. 'I can't believe we've been here 'til night-time!' I said, holding Amber's arm as well as I could in an outfit so layered that it literally did not let my own arms touch my sides.

As we headed, floating, towards the main exit, I noticed the same guy who had smiled at us as we'd entered lean towards the edge of his make-up counter. He literally pulled up a chair. And put his chin in his hands like a child watching TV.

'How odd that he's not smiling,' I thought as I craned my head back to look at him. It was at that point that the store's alarm system started blaring. BEEP BEEP BEEP BEEP.

They needn't really have used the alarm, because security was more than prepared for us. Judging by the number of them at the door, and the speed with which they moved, they had been waiting a while. Boy, were we worth the wait. The minute we crossed the threshold of the store, the team stopped us getting any further, and whisked us immediately to the security room upstairs. Still, we didn't understand why our 'friends' would be doing this to us. They basically owed us the clothes, and anyway – we had been so discreet about it! Then, we saw the security camera footage.

I don't remember much about this part of the evening, but I do remember feeling very confused when I saw the grainy black and white shots of Amber and me walking around the store. There were cameras everywhere – of course there were, it was a huge luxury goods emporium – so there was plenty of footage of our big afternoon out. There were moments I had no recollection of at all. For example, the way that we had come out of the dressing room and started just putting things on in the middle of the store. In front of everyone, staff and customers alike. We had stopped bothering with the formalities long ago, preferring to loop scarves and jewellery over each other in full view.

I would love to be able to tell you that I felt terrible shame at this point, but I don't remember feeling a thing. I suppose maybe I was a little puzzled as to why our 'friends' in the store let us get as far as we did. Maybe they never liked us at all, and they had been waiting for a chance to stitch us up. Maybe they didn't really know how to approach us as they could see how out of our minds we were. Maybe a manager somewhere just felt like teaching staff and customers a lesson on what they wouldn't put up with. But the evidence was undeniable. The tapes aside, we had tried to leave the store covered in unpaid-for goods, tags dangling from every part of us.

Mostly, I was numb: numb from the drink, numb from the drugs, and numb from the shock of realising that perhaps the good times were about to end. The edges blurred further and further at this point. Amber's dad was called to come and get us and I think I recall him arriving. But the next thing I know was that I woke up handcuffed to a hospital bed.

I have never asked, and I don't want to know, but I have no idea what happened to me or how I behaved between my seeing those security tapes and my waking up. I had no idea where I was. My surroundings were entirely unfamiliar and Amber was nowhere to be seen. I felt horrendous. Imagine the worst hangover you have ever had. That feeling was just one fingernail's-worth of how horrific I felt when I came to. Shaky, dehydrated, sick, panicked. After all, I reasoned, I was someone who needed daily medication. No wonder I felt bad if I'd missed a dose.

I tried to move. The handcuffs meant I couldn't get out

of bed to try and find a member of medical staff to help me. I called out until someone came, and begged to be allowed to make a phone call. Obviously I did not want my parents finding out about this. I knew I was in trouble, big legal trouble. But I thought it was about the 'shopping' – it didn't occur to me that what we had done had possibly had serious implications for my health, and my sanity. All I knew was that I needed my meds.

So I called the guy on the crew who had been so helpful getting us so many of our meds. He was a lovely guy, not a sleazy evil pusher type like the dealers I had come across when it was meth I needed to get hold of. He was a sweet, friendly guy. He was incredibly kind when he heard my voice, and told me what had happened to us. The story of our arrest had been on the news, because of its connection to the show.

Still the implications of what I had done to myself had not hit home. I needed my medication. This was not about fun, it was about getting myself 'healthy' again to deal with the legal stuff that was surely heading my way.

'Can you go to my condo and get me my meds? They're in my nightstand, in a brown paper bag. I don't know how long I am going to be in hospital, and I really need them. Please come and get them to me, please.'

My pleading worked and our crew buddy said he would try to do this. But while I was waiting for him to arrive I was told that as I was awake, it was time for me to leave the hospital and go where I belonged: jail. I was terrified, especially as it seemed beyond the point of my parents not finding out. It was some hours before the transportation was ready for me, but the hospital needed back the bed I had been in, so I was put in a hallway, with shackles and handcuffs on. The shackles were unbelievably painful. I know they're not built for comfort, but they jammed right into my ankle bone, and they were so heavy they pulled my leg down whatever position I was in. This, on top of what must have been the early stages of some drug withdrawal, meant that just as I was being kicked out of hospital I was starting to feel I needed it most.

Eventually a vehicle arrived – I don't even know if it was a car, a truck, a bus. When I got to the jail I was feeling worse than ever, as well as being utterly terrified. On arrival they did a sort of coat check on me. I had no idea where my bag or my purse were by now. But I was still forced to give the guards all of my piercings, my belly button ring, all of my clothes and even my shoes. I was handed a prison jumpsuit to put on, and pointed in the direction of a communal cell with a heap of blankets in one corner and a heap of thin mattress pads in another. The guard pointed to me to get one of each. The mattress pads were as light as yoga mats, but the blankets were one of the worst things I had ever felt. They were made from weird wiry wool, as if it were moose hair or something similar. There were spikes that dug into my hands instantly; I couldn't even imagine putting one over my body in the state I was in. But the first challenge was to lift one. I was simply too weak to do it, so it was only a matter of seconds before the guard started shouting at me, 'Don't drag it! Don't drag it!'

For the next three days the guards were all vile to me. I'm not surprised. These were local guys, and someone like me, in there for what I had done, was never really going to win their sympathy. I was led to a cell and left alone. I asked where Amber was and was simply told not to worry about that right now. In all the time I was there, I don't remember eating a thing, or using the bathroom once. I don't know if it simply didn't happen (I wouldn't be surprised) or if my brain has just blocked it out (I wouldn't be surprised by that either). It was an extremely traumatic time. What was happening to my body chemically, combined with where I was and the total lack of information that I had about my circumstances, meant that I was in a state of panic and terror for pretty much every single hour I spent there. I thought a thousand dark thoughts about what I had done, about what my parents must be thinking, doing, feeling, and about where on earth things would go from here.

Finally, at the end of the third day, right before bedtime, the guards came to get me a final time. They took me outside in handcuffs and led me towards a blue jeep. Then, they simply unlocked my handcuffs and pointed to the jeep door. 'You are going to the airport,' was all I was told. Still scared, I opened the jeep door, and saw that it was the head of transportation from *Lost*. Amber was in there too. The entire contents of our condo was packed up and stacked in the back of the jeep. All of our belongings and suitcases were in there. It seemed like years since I had seen them. As soon as I saw Amber I gave her the biggest hug. But beyond that we barely spoke.

'I'm taking you to the airport,' he said. 'And then your moms are picking you up.'

We knew a lot of shit must have gone down. And we knew that the last people we wanted to face right now were our moms. I wanted to run away, but there was nowhere left to go. It was a totally silent car journey after that.

Luckily among my belongings was my brown bag of medication, so by the time we boarded the plane, I at least had the comfort of that. Amber and I barely spoke on the plane. Mostly, we slept, but my brain was whirring with anxiety about what I was going to face when I got to the airport. No one had yet told us what we had been charged with, if indeed any charges had been made. All we knew was that Hawaii wanted us out, and that our parents wanted us out of Hawaii. I tried to imagine what my parents must have been through these last few days. Who had told them where I was? What had they had to do to get us home? What did they know about what state I was in? Had they seen the footage from Neiman Marcus? These questions, and many more, swarmed my brain whatever I tried to do to shut it up. It was almost unbearable. But it was nothing compared to seeing my mom's face when we finally did land.

We left the airport with our red travel blankets over our heads, desperate to avoid anyone taking photographs of us after hearing our story on the news. As promised, both of our mothers were there at Arrivals. The four of us drove silently to Amber's house where my mom had parked her car. We got out and moved straight into her car before driving home together. During this journey, after having seen the pain and disappointment on my mom's face, I reached a fresh new low. I realised that the guilt of what I had done was overwhelming me. To have been on the news, getting arrested. Something like this had never, ever happened to anyone in our family. It felt like the most shaming thing in the entire universe, and my parents had done nothing to deserve it but love and support me all of my life.

It started to seem very clear. It would be better for the family if I wasn't there. I would surely keep doing this; it would get worse and worse if I wasn't stopped. I was in physical pain and I was in emotional pain, but worst of all, I was causing others so much pain. This time – unlike ever before – there were no reprimands from my mom. She was just utterly silent, as if grief-stricken. They had had enough, the whole family had had enough. They are such kind people and I was just destroying them. The way I saw it that night, they would all be better off without me. I didn't want to be alive any more as it was only going to cause more pain for everyone.

When we got home, my mom started to take my bags out of the car and I headed inside and went up to my bedroom. I sat on the edge of my bed for a minute, and realised that this, at last, was the end of the road. I walked slowly, silently back downstairs. My mom and I were the only ones in the house. She was in the kitchen. I approached her at the kitchen counter and looked at her, willing myself not to cry.

'Mom,' I said, my voice trembling. 'I am not kidding. I want to kill myself. If you do not take me to hospital right now, I am going to do it. I am really sorry to cause you more trouble, but I just know what a disappointment I am. And it's never-ending. I can see that life would simply be so much better for you guys if I weren't here. I am serious.'

'Okay, Stephanie,' she replied, her voice as low and quiet as mine. 'I understand. I am going to take you right now. Let's go pack a bag.'

My mom came upstairs with me and helped me to find an overnight bag. I was sobbing and sobbing, a combination of relief, fear and pain. I sat on the bed, surrounded by the trinkets and mementoes of my childhood. Toys, photographs, souvenirs. It all served only to remind me just how much

I had messed up. My life should have been perfect, I had been offered whatever opportunities I wanted. And instead of making it as anyone or anything, I had destroyed everything. Sitting there trying to get pyjamas out of drawers I hadn't opened for months was truly one of the absolute lowest points of my life. And let's not forget I'd already attempted suicide once.

My mom left the room for only a moment – to call the hospital and say that we were coming – when I remembered that I would need to bring some medication for the stay. I found a purse that I remembered from last time I was in UCLA, as you needed to have a bunch of quarters to use the payphone there. I wanted to be better prepared this time. Really well prepared. Because that little purse also had a hidden little zipper pocket, and into that I shoved a bunch of Vicodin. These were still a narcotic, but a less powerful one. It was about eight or ten pills, just enough for the first few days, I figured.

We headed to the hospital while my mind was still a mess – veering between the total conviction that suicide was the wisest, and probably only, option for me right now, and planning for how I was going to keep my supply of medication up while I was on the ward. When we arrived we had to wait in ER for a couple of hours until they had a bed for me on the A South ward. At last, I was shown to the ward, and a large room with about six beds.

Once I was there and my mom had filled in the paperwork and been reassured enough that it was okay for her to leave, I felt more alone than I ever have done. I had those few Vicodin, but realistically they barely touched the sides, given the size of the problem that I was now dealing with. As far as the hospital were concerned, I was a suicide risk, having something of a breakdown, but they didn't realise the volume of drugs I had been taking, or the amount of time that I had been doing it for. No one did.

In short, they did not have what I needed to get well. I wanted to die, and no one had addressed that with me. No one (least of all me) seemed to have any handle on the fact that I was dealing with both depression and addiction. That this was about eight years of misdiagnoses and bad friendships and wrong choices and easily available opiates mixed together into one big mess. One thing was not going to get better unless everything was seen as the same problem – although of course I couldn't see it like that at that point either.

I still would have preferred to die. But seeing my mom's face at the hospital that night had made me realise that maybe – maybe – I should not cause them any more immediate pain. Nevertheless it was a really, really rough few days. Apart from anything else, I simply couldn't stop crying. I just sobbed, day and night. I barely slept, and wept whenever anyone tried to even talk to me. My mom came to visit the first morning for initial meetings with doctors and I could not get a word out. Only tears would come.

In turn, my mom sobbed too. She just wanted to do whatever she could, so she was pleading with me, 'We're not mad, we love you, we just want you to be well, we just want you to be happy.' She repeated these things to me again and again through her own tears, which only made me sadder, to realise how much hurt I was continuing to inflict on her. I felt I was a terrible person.

The hospital just saw someone suicidal who had stopped eating so they forced me to drink chicken broth the whole time. 'It'll make you feel better,' they said, but I knew that it was going to take so much more than that. In fact, in those few early days, I didn't believe that anything could make me feel better, ever.

What no one had really observed was that guilt, shame and tiredness aside, I was basically going through heroin withdrawals. It was constant, never-ending pain, all over. Imagine when you have been to the gym, or a really long run, and worked your body to its absolute limit, until you can take no more. Or imagine the worst flu you have ever had, when even lying down aches your body where your flesh hits the sheet. Imagine the deepest desperation you have ever felt, and then the fieriest anger that has ever burned through you. Imagine feeling all of these things, as well as a strength and determination that means you could punch a wall and go straight through it. Well, that, that is what a tiny fraction of opiate withdrawals feels like. Every sensation and emotion that I had used drugs to suppress, over the years, was rearing up, screaming at me all at the same time. For a moment, I thought I might actually be turning into the Hulk.

This wasn't a rehab facility; they didn't have the equipment to deal with the trouble I was in. My blood tests had not yet come back, on this first day, and no one was really on the lookout for signs of opiates in me as it was something that had not come up in my history before. I was given some sleeping pills to try and help me to get some rest, but really, they did nothing. It was this stalemate situation that led to the real craziness beginning.

I had run out of the few Vicodin I had managed to smuggle in to help me with those first few days, so now the withdrawal was at its most intense. It had been five or six years of one thing then another in my body. The meth, the coke, the weed, the pills, it had never really ended. Now I was somewhere where I couldn't access them any more, and I had a feeling I was going to be here for a few days, or even a few weeks. I was there for months. So, if I was going to cope (I know, it makes no sense) I was going to need my medication. I needed painkillers, fast. And what's the best way to get painkillers if you're already in a hospital, and no one's giving them to you? Create more pain.

My ingenious plan was to injure myself, as severely as I could manage. With perfect clarity I told myself, 'The only way I can stop feeling this pain, is if I create a new one. I will have to break my arm . . .' That way, they had to give me some drugs, surely.

I looked over at the girl in the bed next to me. Liza was about my age and seemed like the kind of person who would support my fantastic plan.

'I think I am going to put my desk on top of my bed and then jump off both, on to the edge of that chair, so that I can snap my wrist,' I whispered.

'You're not going to do that,' she replied.

Not as impressed or supportive as I would have hoped. Instead of defeating me, her dissing my plan only fuelled my rage and determination.

I hauled the desk round from beside my bed, and pulled it up on to the mattress itself. It was incredibly wobbly, but I just needed the height to get a decent fall. I lined the chair up in front of the bed itself. The plan was just to snap my wrist. Nothing too fancy, just a nice clean break, which would ensure a supply of pain medication.

I climbed up on to my bed, aware that the others in the ward were now watching, wondering if I was really going to see this through.

'There is no way you are going to jump,' called a voice. I climbed up on to the desk itself, wobbling horribly on the bed.

'Ignore her, she's not going to jump,' said someone else.

'I really don't want to jump,' I thought to myself. But the way I saw it in that moment, I was sick of letting people down. I was the girl who always said she was going to do something, then never did. I had been an endless disappointment, never finishing anything, never getting a single thing done.

'Well,' I told myself, 'today's the day I'm going to change. I'm finally going to see something through!'

Also, I really wanted those pills. The room swayed beneath me. The chair down there looked like something that actually might be able to break my arm. The laughter from the others in the room got a little louder. Looking back now, I can't believe that it was me on that desk. I can see the room as if from an outsider's perspective, me up there, staring down at the other patients. My life seems so, so far from that moment that it seems mad it ever happened. But in that moment, I was one hundred per cent sure that I was following the only reasonable course of action. I paused, terrified at what I was about to do.

Then, as I saw Liza in the bed next to me giggling at my perilous position, and I felt those pains throughout my entire body as I extended it to a standing position, I realised that I had to jump. So jump I did.

I screamed as I hit the chair, and then the floor.

'Liza! Please! Get help! Go and tell them I'm hurt,' I yelled, unsure whether I wanted help with my arm or if I just wanted those pills to come as soon as possible. Liza ran out of the room – in which no one was laughing any more – and seconds later three nurses came running in.

Christmas photo
with my sister
Kristin and
brother Spencer,
1990.

Annual Spring
Break family ski
trip to Deer Valley.

Hanging out with my pony Kiwi.

After the show with my ribbons.

I was a very competitive horse back rider. This is me riding in a Trancas horse show.

My mom was always class mom at school. This is us on Valentine's Day at Crossroads school.

Another Christmas photo 1991.

At my middle school graduation with Spencer holding the flowers and card he brought me. He was the best big brother.

Taking selfies on the beach with my dad last year (he's wearing my hat as a joke).

My dad and me at dinner in Kauai on a family vacation.

My high school graduation from Crossroads.

Easter photo with my whole family at the Beach Club.
My mom was trying out dark brown hair.

My best friend Lo and I at the MTV music awards.

Group shot of the cast and creators of the Hills at our series finale party.

'Stephanie! Stephanie! What's happened?' they asked, panicked.

'I fell out of bed!' I shrieked, rolling around in agony – both real and over-dramatised. 'I've broken my arm! I need help!'

At this point I didn't even know if my arm was actually broken or not. I did know that there had been a loud crack and I was somehow in even more pain than before. I was swept up into a wheelchair amidst much drama and confusion, and whisked straight to X-ray. As the wheelchair rattled down the corridor, I sat there clutching my arm, silently thinking to myself, 'You genius, you nailed it. You absolutely nailed it.'

Except of course I hadn't, because it was perfectly obvious to the staff that I couldn't possibly have fallen out of my bed. Why? Because I couldn't even have been in my bed: my desk was still on it. No one believed for a minute that I had fallen, only I hadn't realised that yet. When did I realise? When I came out of X-ray, and was told solemnly that I had indeed fractured my arm . . . and was given a couple of kids' ibuprofen for the pain.

I sat in the wheelchair waiting to be taken back to the ward. It hadn't worked. Nothing was working. I had withdrawal pain, severe depression, and a broken arm. And nothing but two infant ibuprofen for support.

I guess this is what people call hitting rock-bottom. Because I really didn't have much further to fall once I realised that I was being wheeled to an entirely different wing. 'Where are you taking me?' I asked, panicked.

'I'm afraid we have now got you in a 72-hour hold,' I was told. 'You are going to A West.'

Instead of being taken to my previous bed, desk and all, I was now being led to an entirely different wing of the hospital, and being put under the State of California's 72-hour hold, made infamous by Britney Spears. This is when things stop being merely medical, but become legal as well. The hospital decided that as I had broken my own arm, and was so easily prepared to commit such harm to myself, I was also a potential risk to others.

I didn't quite see it that way yet, as I was still silently fuming that I had not been given the drugs I was craving, but this was the best thing that could have happened to me. A West ward is the kind of place where a nurse watches your every move. There are no more trips to the bathroom alone, there is no more taking any medication without a nurse checking under your tongue that it has been swallowed. The days of nice food, TV, movies and trying to rest in peace are over. It is now *Girl, Interrupted* time. The ward I was now in was like an old-fashioned asylum. The kind of place where a man would suddenly just start screaming in rage at a wall.

That night my parents arrived. They had brought me a California Pizza Kitchen pizza, my childhood favourite. I had still never seen my dad cry yet in his life, but that night he was utterly distraught. My mom was also in pieces, of course.

'Stephanie,' she said quietly. 'We have got to deal with this now. This addiction. It is too much for any of us now.'

'Just get me out of here,' I begged. 'I'll go anywhere, I'll do anything.'

They promised that they would do their best, but a 72-hour hold is legally binding, so I could not just up and leave. It was out of all of our hands for a couple of days. My parents were as desperate to move me as I was desperate to leave, but the hospital's argument was, 'She cannot be moved anywhere until we are sure she will not harm others.' It was no longer a case of 'this is what we think might be best for Stephanie', but had moved on to 'this is what you have to do now'.

Time crawled, but I eventually made it through those seventy-two hours. My sister had just had her first baby, who she brought to meet me. But instead of feeling joy at meeting her firstborn, I simply felt sad that this adorable little creature had to come to a mental hospital to see me. After the few days, I made it back to my original ward, and started to co-operate. I attempted food again, and was prepared to look at some rehab choices. My family and those taking care of me realised at last that I had to be somewhere that could deal with serious drug withdrawals. And in the meantime, I slept. I slept and I slept and I slept. I felt as if I were catching up on all of the sleep that I had been missing out on since high school. Months and months of sleepless nights, years of sleep disrupted by addiction. I slept and I slept and I slept some more. Until one morning, nearly a month later, my mom came to get me and said, 'We're off to rehab.'

'Where are we going?' I asked.

'Houston, Texas,' she replied. And an hour later we were on our way to the airport.

6

For the first time in a long time, I wasn't fighting my situation. I fully accepted it. I was tired of being broken. My mom and I boarded the plane to Houston together, and when we arrived the facility had sent a car to collect us. As we drove up to the centre it was impossible not to notice the high fences surrounding it. This was a lockdown kind of place. A gated estate with no escape. I started to sob, and that in turn started my mom off crying.

'I'm so sorry, Mom, I'm so sorry,' I cried. 'I am sorry I need to be here.'

'Don't worry,' she said. 'It's going to be okay, it's all going to be okay.'

I was scared. And as well as the fear about what was coming next for me, I was incredibly disorientated. I had gone straight from Hawaii to hospital, spending only an hour or so at home in between. And now I was in another state altogether, without having been home again. My mom had packed my bags, not trusting me to come back to my bedroom and do it myself in case I had hidden drugs there. Understandably, she didn't want to take the risk of me getting high before heading to rehab. As a result I had no idea where any of my stuff was. I hadn't seen my phone or Blackberry for weeks, I was totally off radar with no idea of what was going on with any of my friends – if indeed I still had any friends. I had been in such a hole for so long. There is no time to wonder what everyone else is up to when it is taking every ounce of your strength to get through the next ten minutes.

We entered the facility and checked in. There was an immediate sense that there were now some real professionals in charge. Everyone seemed like they absolutely knew what they were doing, and that they'd seen it all before. There was a businesslike briskness about the staff that made me suspect they were unshakeable.

I was shown to my room and made to unpack in front of the team there. They were lovely, very respectful, but it was still humiliating to realise that you had come to a point where you had to be checked like this. I didn't have anything I wasn't allowed, but they did take the shoelaces from my Converse, as it was standard practice not to let anyone have laces. There are some people who still think

94

that all residential rehab facilities are like spa retreats, but this one really wasn't. It was clean and welcoming – and a much more comforting environment than being on a hospital ward – but there was no illusion that this was a holiday.

My room was a twin one, shared with another girl around the same age as me. I had been desperate to have a room to myself but I quickly realised that that was simply not an option. There were six rooms with two of us in each one. I was lucky to have got a place there, so I was happy with being allowed to stay at all. It was simply furnished, like a twin room in a decent B&B.

That first night I couldn't sleep at all. I got undressed silently, in the dark, as my roommate was already asleep, before just lying there with my mind on fire. Who am I? Where am I? What is going to happen to me? But the staff were clearly prepared for this. There was a sort of pre-school atmosphere to the place after dark – if we couldn't get any sleep we were allowed to get out of bed and sit in a communal area with couches where there was a nurse keeping an eye on us. We could help ourselves to milk and cookies, read books and magazines or watch TV. After half an hour or so of lying in the dark, trying to sleep in my new unfamiliar surroundings, I went out to sit on one of those couches. I had butterflies in my stomach like you have at a new job or a new school. Thoughts kept running through my mind. What are they going to make me do tomorrow? Who will I talk to? Will I make any friends? Will they cure me? After a while I finally settled a little. I could feel my heart rate lower and my buzzing mind slowly unwind as I flicked through the selection of books, making a mental note of what I might get around to reading during my stay.

At around 1.00 am the tranquillity was interrupted by a sudden burst of activity coming from the reception area. I could hear beepers going, and several of the staff rushing to the entrance. The main doors opened and two members of staff carried in a young girl whose face was absolutely covered in cuts, scratches and grazes. She was probably only about fifteen or sixteen. They put her into a wheelchair and delicately wheeled her into the facility. As she went past, I could see that she was now wrapped up almost entirely like a mummy, as she had so many injuries. She looked as if she had been hit by a car, and was clearly in a lot of distress.

'Maybe you should head back to bed now,' said the nurse sitting in the area where I was. 'Time to try and get a little sleep.'

'But what's happened to that girl?' I asked, panicked.

'We can't tell you that right now, but I'm sure you'll meet her soon,' was all she would say. 'We have to check-in our new patient now.'

Obviously after something as unsettling as that I barely slept a wink. Who were the other people coming here?

What had they been through? Was I the same as them? As daylight crept in from behind the curtains, I came to realise that yes, maybe I was. Which only served to make me even more anxious about what lay ahead.

Only a couple of hours later one of the staff came in to wake us up, but I begged to be allowed to stay in bed. I was craving a little period of solitude before the day ahead, and mercifully they trusted me and left me for a few hours to catch up on the sleep that I had missed. I couldn't hide forever though, and eventually I headed out to get to know my new home.

The centre was a bit like its own planet, entirely enclosed and pretty much self-sufficient. You couldn't leave, but you never needed to leave, so in time you . . . just stopped thinking about it. The buildings were all purpose-built, around a central area, so it felt like a small university campus or a very specific gated community. One house was for eating disorders, one was for drugs, one was for personality disorders. And while we were all based in one of these houses, we would also cross over to the others during the day for different sessions. Because, as I came to understand, it's pretty rare to have a long-term addiction without developing some sort of quirks around your eating patterns, and it's rare to have a personality disorder without resisting the temptation to self-medicate with some sort of drugs at some point. I learned that I wasn't a complete disaster; it was pretty common.

I was of course in the house where people were being treated for drug addictions, but I spent a fair amount of time in the eating disorder house as well. After all, by the time I arrived, I was still incredibly uncomfortable eating in front of other people, in what seemed to be a sort of throwback from my trying not to eat at all while in UCLA. For the first few days I couldn't eat in the communal cafeteria at all, and just stayed in my room during mealtimes eating fruit, or as little as I could get away with.

I soon learned that our days were very structured, almost like a college student's. We each had a personalised schedule of what we would be doing that day. You had to keep on top of where you were meant to be and when. There was always a check-in, to see how we were feeling that morning, if there was anything we were struggling with or needed extra help with. Then it would be a combination of cognitive behavioural therapy, individual therapy, group therapy, an eating disorder clinic and some sort of fun sport like volleyball breaking it up. And we all wore name-tags, so if a member of staff saw us in a part of the campus where we weren't meant to be, they could immediately check with a colleague and make sure that we were not up to no good.

It was not long into that first day that I found out what had happened to the girl who had arrived in such dramatic fashion the night before: she had thrown herself out of the car bringing her to the facility. Right then, I knew that I was where I needed to be to get myself better. I was shocked that I was considered on the same level as this girl, but in a strange way I was also relieved. The people here were unshakeable, they had seen it all before, and that must mean that they would know how to handle someone like me. They could help me. They could cure me.

I was a little fearful, as this was undeniably a dark, dark place. Somewhere people arrived at the lowest it is possible to get yourself. But instead of trying some crazy scheme, I surrendered to the fact that I was one of those people, and this wasn't just a dark place, but somewhere where we could be mended.

At first I was on some controlled medication to help me with the withdrawals. Every morning I would be handed a few very specific pills, and still had to endure the whole looking under the tongue thing, to make sure that they had been swallowed and not stashed for getting high later by taking a load all in one go. I never tried any tricks, because I was so relieved by the consistently professional sense that everyone in charge knew exactly what I needed, but if I had ever tried to protest I am sure that it would have been met with great calmness. A gentle 'That's not how it works here' was the most I ever heard said when anyone protested, and it usually worked.

After my years of creating drama and pain, these people seemed gently unshockable and all of us who were being treated seemed to understand and respect this. There was no point kicking off, because it wouldn't work. But also, there was no point in hiding what you had done in the past, because that wouldn't get a rise either. After my initial panic about it, the tone that was set started to feel really liberating to be around. I became more and more aware of how lucky I was to have a place here, the longer that I stayed. I was there for three months in the end, and at last I got all the help I needed. I liked the people who were treating me. It felt like they were grown-ups who knew what they were doing. I felt stronger, better, healthier every day.

But, as I said, it wasn't all relaxed chats and spa vibes though. I had so much anger, it would come spiralling out of me in group chats or one-to-ones and then I would have to spend the next day apologising to people for the way I had spoken. I hadn't had a properly clear mind since I was about thirteen, so I hadn't developed emotionally as I should have done. Dealing with this was incredibly tough – I had to catch up with myself, and I lived a few years' worth of teen angst in a few weeks. I would call my poor parents and scream at them, telling them I hated them and I was running away from rehab. Then I would be calmed down, I would talk things through with the counsellors, and then I would call back and be mending bridges.

Of course there were physical effects too. Several years of drug abuse can't just vanish without leaving a physical trace. In rehab you have no vices at all really – apart from cigarettes and caffeine. There were days when I would have to deal with cravings on a minute-by-minute, then hour-by-hour level. The idea of facing an entire day without drugs seemed impossible first thing in the morning, but by breaking it down into these tiny chunks and talking to those around me, I slowly experienced those longings less and less.

Outside in the central area there were a few lounge chairs for people to gather on between their meetings and sessions, and I can quite clearly remember sitting on one with the sun on my face and my eyes closed. I wanted to be thinking about how great it was to be clean, how healthy and happy I was becoming. But I was just fantasising about drugs. I was lost in an imaginative world where I was surrounded by as many of 'my' drugs as I wanted, and I could just keep taking and taking them until at last it was all over. 'At least, if I had had all my drugs, I would be dying happy,' I thought to myself.

When I was in moments like that I honestly believed that they were forever. But they would pass. On the other hand, when I was beginning to feel clear-headed and strong again, a craving would hit me. I learned to accept that these things would come in waves, and not always when I would expect them. And slowly, in time, the gaps between those waves got bigger and bigger.

One of the biggest challenges in rehab was boredom.

When you're spending most of your life high, you lose hours of every day to drugs. Then, once you're clean, you suddenly have all this time . . . and all these extra thoughts. It was exciting, but also overwhelming at times. It also made me crave all sorts of other things. When you're suddenly living in this new life with all this . . . daylight and . . . health, it feels as if there are no ups or downs any more. That's a good thing, but as far as my physical senses were concerned, I wondered if I would ever feel anything again. So I took up all sorts of weird habits just to break the tedium.

I started to smoke clove cigarettes on the recommend-ation of someone else there. Then vanilla or even black cherry cigarettes – whatever could bring a little flavour, or differentness to the day, without affecting my mood too much. And I'm not a soda drinker but I was drinking cherry, vanilla, diet Dr Pepper. Whatever I could get my hands on to make it feel less like it was all water and air and thoughts . . .

As the days went on, I started to get to know my house-mates, and to hear their stories too during group therapies. Often, I would sit there dumbfounded. The first time that I realised, 'Fuck, it wasn't just me who felt like this,' felt like an enormous weight lifted from my shoulders. Slowly I came to see that I hadn't been the only one falling into these destructive patterns or feeling these paralysing emotions. It was honestly a revelation to discover that other people had had these thoughts and done these things, too. I remember sitting there time after time, thinking, 'Yes, that is me. That is how I have felt and I can see now that that is how I have been behaving, too.' Gone were the days of therapists boring me into not saying anything, or other patients only making me hate myself more. Now I saw for the first time that I was not alone, that none of us really are.

Hearing how much worse off than me other people had been was also a massive comfort – not because I wanted them to have suffered, but because it helped me to realise that you're rarely the worst in any situation. There was one guy my age whose entire body was a mass of cutting marks from self-harm, and would be like that for the rest of his life. And hundreds of drug- and alcohol-abuse stories that made mine pale in comparison. Until I reached this place I had never met another person who had felt – or been – suicidal before. I was the only person I had known who had actually seen something like that through, and I had felt powerfully alone as a result.

It was such a feeling of relief that they had figured out what was wrong with me and that it could be dealt with, that there was a strategy. To finally hear that there wasn't some strange secret thing inside of me making me behave all wrong. The process my therapists used to help me to see this was really interesting – I could sense them gently checking that there wasn't anything I was hiding from them, too ashamed to say. 'How were your parents with you when you were little?' they would ask. 'Were they strict? Did it ever feel like maybe they were a little too strict?' They poked and prodded, trying to make sure that there were no darker reasons I might have turned to drugs. I would just laugh in frustration, for days on end. 'I'm sorry guys, I just can't give you that stuff!' I'd say. 'My parents are the nicest guys in the world – if anything that's the problem.' And so it was. It was the guilt that had been killing me.

'Why isn't Stephanie happy?' I would feel the question rear up again and again from the moment I hit adolescence.

'Why can't I feel perfect like them?' I would feel in answer.

'How can she possibly want more, need more?' I would be sure they were thinking . . .

Everyone in my family had always been happy. We really were the Californian dream family. Any upset or pain always seemed to have been caused by me – I was the freak, the suicidal freak ruining the good times for the perfect family. And I had no idea why I was like that, why I had had these impulses or why I was seemingly the only imperfect one. Over time – and thanks to the endless patience of the staff and the others at the facility – I learned that there wasn't something specific that had 'happened' to make me like this. It was a chemical imbalance in my brain – that is all that severe depression is.

And I had tried to 'treat' it with years and years of drugs, which had of course only made things so much worse. I had spent years trying to cut myself off from hearing what my brain wanted to tell me, and finally I grew the confidence to engage with it.

Some people are just a bit different. They don't always fit in with what everyone else looks like, or feels like, or where they are. They might be a bit more fragile. They might approach life differently. But they are not broken, they are just a bit different. And there are loads of us like this, fucking up all over the world for all sorts of different reasons! Those sessions were the first time I looked around the room and thought, 'I'm not a freak. No one is.'

Once I was ready to leave, my parents came to pick me up, as I was moving to a sober-living facility. At last, I was one hundred per cent committed to the idea of getting healthy and staying that way. For the first time in years it sounded like a good idea. I wasn't fighting the idea of not taking drugs any more. And I felt so much lighter. Happiness began to creep back in.

We didn't even go back to my parents' house on my arrival back in California. Instead we went straight to a place called Clearview in Venice, where I lived for a further two months. There were twelve of us in the facility, living together in a large house. Again, it was something like a college atmosphere. Apart from, of course, the sober living . . .

We were drug tested before bed every day, and we spent our daytimes doing more therapy, beach yoga and Alcoholics Anonymous or Narcotics Anonymous meetings. Once the staff had approved it, we were allowed to have access to our cars to drive ourselves to meetings, and then once we were doing really well we were allowed to make trips to visit family and to reintegrate with friends. I was really, really happy during this time, as well as feeling healthy for the first time as an adult. I got back to reading the books I had loved in Paris, with my old pal Freud making a reappearance. My mind was clearer, able to focus on things beyond getting through the next hour or two. I could think beyond myself and my own problems for the first time in years. Instead, I read about psychology and philosophy, about what other people's brains were up to. I remember one afternoon reading a book on borderline personality disorder and my mind boggling that anyone could have told me that was my problem. That was never me, even if my behaviour on drugs had led people to believe it.

In Texas I had had absolutely no contact with anyone at all, apart from my immediate family. Now that I was back in LA, and I had earned my phone back in the eyes of Clearview, I was starting to get back in touch with people. Old LA friendships were starting to resurface . . . but not all of them.

One of the most important lessons that I learned in rehab

was that in order to stay sober you have to get rid of absolutely any friend that you have done drugs with. If I ever gave anyone any advice on how to stay clean, it would be that: you have to cut those friendships dead. I have still never spoken to anyone who I partied with in those years before rehab. You can't even see people like that during the day. No one who has had an addiction is that strong, no one.

Nothing is going to change if you don't change the negative people you surround yourself with. You simply cannot get clean if you are in the same place with the same people. The thing about other addicts who are still using drugs or alcohol is that they don't want people around them to get clean – it just makes them feel guilty. I know this, because I used to be one of them. If you're taken to jail in the middle of the night and you are terrified of everything and everyone around you, it's not going to be your addict friends who bail you out in the morning. They'll be sleeping it off, and they won't want to think about why it was you and not them this time.

These days, I don't have to think about actively trying to avoid drugs as I did back then. It has got to the point where I just love and respect life too much to be trying to miss out on any of it. I want to stay alive and healthy for as long as possible to get the most out of it all. I want my body to keep going as long as it can, in as good a shape as it can. Apart from the harm that drugs themselves can do, they are cut with such scary things. There isn't even any weird romance about taking any particular drug, and how it might represent your personality, as half the time that's not even what you've taken. You don't know what it is! And because I'm no longer thinking about drugs as much, I'm no longer seeing signs of them as much. I don't have any friends who do them any more, so if anyone around me is taking drugs, I wouldn't notice it – it's simply not a topic of conversation around me.

Those months in rehab and at Clearview were not easy, but they changed my life forever. What I had resisted for so long – change – was exactly what I needed. It took a long time, six years. And I was only able to see it through because of the support of my family, but eventually I was clean, and strong enough to live a life beyond rehab. At last, I had boundaries, I had a renewed relationship with my family, and I was ready for a fresh start. I planned to start studying at FIDM again, and was up for an entirely renewed friendship group – and one that was fun, not a bunch of seedy nocturnal addicts.

Mainly, I was spending time with my old friend Alishea. I didn't meet her until I was about seventeen, and she had never had a drug problem or been into that scene at all. When I got back from Hawaii and Texas I was too ashamed to call her. I knew she would never understand how things had got so bad, and I felt terrible for keeping the extent of my problems – and their repercussions – from her. We had completely lost touch when I literally bumped into her at the Coffee Bean in Pacific Palisades. It was like a weight had been lifted from me.

'Stephanie, I've heard rumours,' she said. 'I've been so worried but didn't know how to get in touch.'

I confessed that I had been too embarrassed to call. I am so glad that I did just tell her the truth that day, as it meant we were soon close friends again. She is still one of my best friends today, and has always been so supportive of me. When I first left Clearview, she would come to meetings with me. It sounds a little odd, but I would mostly go to Alcoholics Anonymous meetings back then. It was simply a practical decision – there were more of them than Narcotics Anonymous meetings – and the process and the discussion about surviving addiction was always the same.

These days, I am partial to the odd glass of champagne, red wine or vodka soda. But it's pretty rare. I have never had a problem with alcohol, and nor have I ever really craved it. I didn't drink it at all when I came out of rehab and then left Clearview. After all that time not drinking in Texas, and then spending so many evenings at AA hearing about how destructive it can be to other people, it just seemed like the sensible and supportive thing to do not to drink. I was also very aware that people who had been in those AA meetings might see me with a glass of wine at the table one dinner time and worry about me, not knowing my full history. I didn't want to put temptation in anyone's way either, after having had the struggles I'd had.

When the new term started I returned to FIDM to continue the fashion studies course I had dropped in order to go to Hawaii, and in the evenings I would either attend meetings or catch up with old friends. Another person I reconnected with was Roxy, my friend from school. She was also not drinking so we would sometimes go to a meeting together. After a while we got a little routine going where we'd meet every Tuesday night and go out. We'd have a nice dinner together somewhere and then go to a club. We'd just be drinking Red Bull but we wouldn't care as we'd be with each other. I never wanted to be caught with my defences down as a result of drinking and then find myself talking to someone with drugs to spare.

It felt good to be out, to get dressed up and hear music again! Having a new, improved social life felt fantastic. I loved the trust I found in the people who had stuck by me, and felt relief at not being in touch with those people who had been a negative part of my darkest times. LA at that time, at that age, felt like a magical place where the thing you least expected could happen. And, just as I was ready to make friends and start a new life, something did indeed come along.

When it was time to leave Clearview, they had a little 'graduation' for us. I'm so glad that they did this as it had by now been so long since I had been at home – months in

Hawaii, hospital, Texas and Clearview had come to nearly a year – and it felt like a huge deal to be heading to my parents' house to start afresh. There were about eight of us leaving, and we had the chance to invite our friends and family to a ceremony that we'd all attend. Each of us in turn was invited to stand up in the middle of the group, to say a little about our experience, what we'd changed about ourselves, what we were sorry about and what our aims for the future were. It was a chance to look back and also to look forward.

My dad, who, as you know by now is the nicest man in the world, but also one who will always avoid confrontation, has still only ever cried in front of me once. And it was that day. When it was his turn he got into the centre of the circle to speak and started crying. He just let go, he couldn't even talk.

'Steph, I love you,' was as much as he could manage. Every time he opened his mouth to speak he cried more. It seemed that he simply couldn't talk about everything that we had been through, and for once in his life he just needed to feel it. But that 'I love you' was all I needed. Those thirty seconds were the final turning point for me. I sat there and thought, 'I will never make him cry, ever again. I have taken them to hell and back, and now it's over. Never again.'

7

While I'd been in rehab I'd had little or no contact with the outside world. What was going on with my friends, with popular culture, with celebrities – it all became a faraway mystery to me. But that didn't mean that things had stopped happening. Quite the opposite, in fact. 2006 and 2007 were a particularly weird period for celebrity in California. I was so cut off that I didn't know it at the time, but while I was dealing with my problems, there were several female celebrities going through similar things and being hounded in the media for it. Britney, Lindsay Lohan, Paris Hilton: Los Angeles was the epicentre of it and it seemed your fate could go either way. There is so much pressure on young girls to be chasing this idea of perfection, and it was something even the celebrities themselves were doing. No one could live up to the dream; we were all buckling under the pressure. You don't have to live up to being the perfect image that the magazines or TV shows want you to be. Those people don't really even exist. Everyone is fighting their own battle. And in the midst of this, while I'd been busy telling myself that Spencer didn't have a 'real' job he'd actually been working pretty hard – and become a part of popular culture himself.

Back in the early 2000s, reality TV was only a career option for two families in the world: the Osbournes and the newly married Jessica Simpson and Nick Lachey – and all of them were famous as music-industry stars already. These days it's completely different, but back then you had to be known to get on a show.

Or that's what everyone thought until Spencer came along. He didn't get why the Osbournes were so interesting. Just because they live in a mansion in Beverly Hills? Boring! I have a friend with a way bigger mansion, he thought. And he did.

Since childhood Spencer and Brody Jenner had been best friends. Born a week apart, they had grown up together in Malibu, spending time in the surf, goofing around at sport after school, and later getting into girls and all the other naughtiness that teenage boys do. But Brody's dad Bruce and his mom Linda Thompson had got a divorce when he was about three years old, and Bruce then went on to marry Kris Kardashian, which meant he really wasn't around so much. Linda remarried when Brody and his brothers were kids, and her new husband David Foster was a sixteen-time Grammy winner, who had been nominated for Oscars, and worked with acts from Chicago to Michael Bublé. He also wrote the theme to *St Elmo's Fire*. He even discovered The Corrs. He was a really busy guy, one of the absolutely biggest players in the music industry. So my dad became a sort of uncle figure to Brody. Whenever he had good news, it was my dad he'd call.

On top of this, David and Linda often worked together, including writing the song 'I Have Nothing' from the soundtrack to *The Bodyguard*. Linda used to go out with Elvis, and her brother was his bodyguard – the whole thing always struck me as perfect.

So their house was big. Really big. It wasn't even really a house – more of an estate. A 22-acre estate, and a $40 million mansion *in Malibu*. You can kind of see Spencer's point. The Osbournes' house was okay, but this house was amazing. And it was filled with really good-looking young guys.

Spencer, with his unstoppable confidence, decided to make his own show. One better than the Osbournes'. Some people might have thought that was aiming a little high, given what a huge hit that show was, but details like that only seem to have spurred him on. He called Brody and said, 'Do you want to be a reality star?' and he just said, 'Hahahaaa.' Understandably. But Spencer (of course) persuaded him that he was serious, and after not too long got the 'Okay, let's do it' he was after.

Spencer being Spencer, he had no doubt that things would all work out, so he dropped out of college and bought a camera. The same guy who had been so sure his childhood pranks would work out was taking things up a notch! The next day he went to the Foster mansion and started filming. He basically moved in, and just taped whatever Brody and his brothers were doing. The combination of laddish pranks and glamorous parties, all taking place in this gorgeous house, was perfect. It was just the same kind of note that *The Osbournes* and *The Newlyweds* had struck, but as if made for teenage boys.

Once filming started David was always yelling at Spencer to get out of the house, telling him he was causing chaos and so on, but Spencer's response was always the same. 'No way! We're making a TV show here! For Fox!' Sometimes a bit of confidence really can get you wherever you want to go.

Because he did indeed sell the show *The Princes of Malibu* to Fox TV, on the basis of a five-minute cut he'd made using iMovie on his laptop. For $4 million. At twenty-two years old he had his own show and an executive producer credit to his name. When the time came for filming the whole series, Fox only asked for one big change: more Spencer.

When he was no longer needed for filming as a voice

behind the camera, Spencer was thinking he would no longer appear, but Fox thought quite the opposite. 'You need to stay on this show to have David yelling at you,' was what they told him. He kept his exec producer credit, but had a new role in front of the camera as Brody's goofy, trouble-making pool house friend. The guy who was always staying over and instigating mischief.

Fox filmed an entire series of the show, but there was one unforeseen snag in Spencer's master plan. A few days after the first episode aired, Linda and David filed for divorce, after twenty-four years of marriage. Fox told Spencer, 'We wanted a family show, but now there's no family.' Only a couple of episodes aired, and it looked as if the lads' careers as reality TV stars were over before they had started.

Nothing could have been further from the truth. Of course it looked as if Spencer had gone from being on the cusp of being a multi-millionaire to having to go back to college like the rest of us. But by now MTV had aired *Laguna Beach: The Real Orange County*, and its success meant that they were following its star Lauren Conrad to Los Angeles. (I was still blissfully oblivious to *The Hills*, not realising it was carrying on the story, as I'd been in Texas with no TV and no phone.)

Spencer realised that they would be filming Lauren and her friends in and around LA. Determined not to give up on his dream, he thought this could be a way of getting on to the show. By the end of season one he had caught the producers' attention and met one of its stars, Heidi Montag. She saw from day one that he was a source of mayhem but a lot of fun too, though it didn't stop her falling in love with him, and by the time I was out of rehab they were a couple, and Spencer's new career was in its early stages.

There was no way to tell how big *The Hills* was going to become. I had watched a little bit of *Newlyweds: Nick and Jessica* and *The Simple Life* before heading to Hawaii and rehab. I enjoyed them both, especially *The Simple Life* which I thought was so funny. I knew Nicole Richie and Paris Hilton too – not well like I knew my small group of school friends – but I had been seeing them around in the same clubs for years. It was kind of a friends-of-friends thing. They were far from must-see TV though. These days I'm on the sofa ready and waiting for the *TOWIE* credits on a Sunday night, but back then if I was in and fancied a little junk TV I'd watch, but I was usually out. I wasn't organising my life around the schedules – no one was. And I certainly didn't think I'd be on one of the shows any time soon.

I had been hanging out with Spencer and his new girl-friend Heidi for months by the time my chance to step in front of the cameras came around. I adored Heidi from the minute I met her; she is the sweetest person I have ever met. Initially Spencer set us up on a 'girl date' together, and soon we were close. Because of there being no access to TV in rehab, I met her with no preconceptions, never having seen a single episode of *The Hills*. We never didn't get on, and during the year after I came home from rehab and Clearview we spent a lot of time at my parents' house, or with Spencer, getting to know each other. She was kind and understanding about everything I had been through in the previous year or so, she knew I was still quite delicate after getting out of rehab, and just getting used to socialising again. You don't forget that easily about someone when you've been through the sort of time that I had.

As our friendship developed, I had heard all about Lauren Conrad. The original premise of the show had been that it would follow Lauren and her friend Heidi as they pursued their dreams of working in fashion and PR. Originally, they were both at FIDM (while I had been away and in rehab), but I soon learned that Heidi had left pretty early on for a cool job at Bolthouse PR where she still worked. She was involved in event management, which sounded to me like access to all the best parties. Lauren was still pursuing the fashion dream.

But it certainly seemed that there was now a lot of bad blood between Heidi and Lauren, and it didn't take long for me to gather that Spencer was at the bottom of it all. The girl I was told about was cruel, judgmental Lauren, who was being so mean to Heidi simply because she didn't like Spencer. I knew the show was doing well and that they suddenly had great-seeming lives, so I was just happy to go along with what I heard. And it really didn't seem that weird when Spencer and Heidi pitched the idea of me featuring in the show because it was pretty clear that Heidi was no longer hanging out with Lauren as much.

'You should come on the show!' Heidi had said.

'Yeah,' Spencer had agreed. 'Now that Lauren won't talk to Heidi any more, you can go to lunch and be her Hills buddy. I'm going to make a call . . .'

'Sure, that sounds fun,' was all I had really said, not believing anything would come of it. But the next I heard was one of the producers following up on Spencer's suggestion and wondering if I would be interested in having a trial scene. I was going to be invited to the Opera nightclub, where the whole gang was going to be having a big night out. At first I just wanted the chance to defend my brother, who was already building something of a reputation as a bit of a bad guy on the show. But this was huge – I knew that this was an incredible opportunity for me for a career, as well as an invitation to some of the most exclusive parties in Hollywood. Already for the cast members *The Hills* wasn't just a job, but a way of life. After all, if the aim of the show was to follow the lives of young people with incredible, aspirational lifestyles, well – you had to have one. And by now Heidi and Spencer certainly did – the show had made them very wealthy very fast.

I knew this was just a trial appearance, and that if I didn't make any impact, there would be no more *The Hills* for me. So the first thing I did was head out shopping for my debut outfit. I was such a total dork about it. There was really only one place I considered going: the Beverly Center, which is a huge eight-storey shopping centre with everything from Louis Vuitton to Forever 21 in it. It's featured in Bret Easton Ellis novels and Grand Theft Auto games. Basically, it's shopping heaven. And to be there with a bona fide reason to find a killer dress – it was the dream.

I spent all afternoon trying on various outfits, and each time trying to talk to the sales staff about how I needed something for 'my debut TV appearance'. Every time I said those words, I expected everyone to gasp and drop what they were doing to look at me. It was like I had forgotten I was in Hollywood, though. Everyone says they're looking for something for a TV appearance when they're shopping in the Beverly Center, from waitresses to award-winning actors, to the housewives of wherever. I don't know who I thought I was kidding.

When I found the dress that was 'the one', I spent ages looking at myself in the store mirrors, trying to imagine myself on screen. I twirled in it, stared back at myself over my shoulder in it, and tried sitting down in it. It was a cute, short dress made with quite a sheer fabric and with a sparkly sequinned empire-line waistband. I still have it today, hanging in my wardrobe in the LA condo that featured in the show. I stepped out into the centre of the store and raised my voice a little.

'So, this is for an appearance on TV,' I said, quickly casting my eyes around the store. Any looks?

'It's going to be on MTV . . .' Nothing. No one cared. Of course they didn't. But I kept going, desperate to tell everyone I was soon going to be on *The Hills*, one of the biggest shows in America. Sadly the producers had already made it very clear to me that to tell a soul would be to lose my chance.

'So, you know, will this sparkly fabric here . . .' (I pointed to the waistline) '. . . affect the cameras at all? Would there be any issues with the cameras? The lighting? The reflections?'

Sadly the response wasn't really what I'd hoped for. A sales assistant said quietly, 'No,' and everyone carried on with their lives. My big TV debut had not had the impact on the Beverly Center that I might have hoped. No one could have cared less.

I was determined to look my best, though, and had a full-on makeover before heading to the club that night. I had a spray tan, a professional make-up artist to do my face, and my hair styled with a middle parting and ringlets around my face (it was 2007 after all . . .). As far as I was concerned, I was going to be breaking hearts all over the country once I hit the screen. Never mind that these days when I see that scene – or any of those early episodes – on TV, I will just turn it off as fast as I can. I can't even look at them with the sound off. They were, shall we say, not my finest hour looks-wise.

By the time the night itself came round I was more stoked up for it than I ever had been for anything. Heidi had been so respectful towards my fragility when I got out of rehab that I fiercely wanted to be protective of her where Lauren was concerned. Let's not forget I had heard nothing but bad things about Lauren, who as far as I was concerned had no reason not to like Spencer beyond jealousy. She just wasn't getting to spend as much time doing single-girl stuff with Heidi. I had also been being told all about how much Brody Jenner, who I had known my entire childhood, had changed. Spencer and Heidi had both lost their very best friends simply as a result of falling in love, and to top things off, it now looked as if Lauren and Brody were seeing each other as well.

When *The Hills* was filmed at clubs they didn't close the venue or have a huge crew there; they tried to do it as unobtrusively as possible. The team would just have a small number of stationary cameras and an area that was slightly cordoned off . . . and let the fireworks begin. Because of course the fireworks always did begin. The first thing I saw when I entered Opera with my old friend Roxy that night and clocked the group of eight or ten of them was that Brody was indeed chatting to Lauren. I felt like a racing dog that had just been let out of a trap. Everything I had been told was true! I could not wait to get at them. But . . . all I could think of to say at first was to spit at them, 'You're on the evil side!' Then I tried to persuade Brody to leave with me. I felt a strange protectiveness, as if I had to get him away from these people who were being mean to my family.

Then, when Lauren confronted me with what my actual problem was, my answer was the truth. 'You hate my brother and that makes me hate you!' I could see the faces of everyone else in the group, looking at each other and mouthing, 'Woah, who is this girl?' Everyone, that is, apart from the ever-unreliable Justin Bobby, who had just moved across the room to chat to a girl who wasn't his girlfriend Audrina for about the millionth time. I had made the impact I wanted to, though, and as the cool air outside the club hit me a while later, it occurred to me that my life might never be the same.

I broke out in hives the minute we were out in the open air. It had been so scary, seeing the light of the cameras and feeling the heat of Lauren and Brody's anger focussed on me. I hadn't got to the club until about 11.45 pm and we were out within a couple of hours, but it had been one of the most intense experiences of my life. The depth of emotion and protectiveness I felt for my family, combined with the music, the smell of booze and the knowledge that I had just opened my life up to all of America felt like an adrenaline rush nothing else had ever been able to give me.

As I drove home, my pulse slowly began to return to normal. The first thing I did was to call Spencer and tell him all about it. His response was as loyal as I would have expected. 'Great job, great job, sister! Thank you!' I could hear Heidi whooping in the background.

'Yeah!' I replied. 'I stood up for my FAMILY!' As I went to bed that night I knew that I had at least achieved that – what the producers would think of my on-screen debut remained to be seen.

I needn't have worried, though, as almost straight away they called me to ask about my availability for doing some further scenes. I explained that I didn't have a job at that point, so I wasn't sure what they would like to follow me doing. But when I mentioned my studies at FIDM they asked for some information about which classes I was taking, then leapt at the chance to shoot me at college.

'Wow,' I thought. 'I must really have some screen presence for them to want to film me taking notes in class or tapping away at a computer.'

I didn't really see how the team at *The Hills* were going to get that much that could be interesting from filming me at this point in my life. After all, I was happy, settled and rested. I was sober, with jail behind me. My family was happy that I was happy and spending time with them. There was no drama to be had. I wondered if maybe it was just an insight into learning about fashion design that they were after. It wasn't even an interesting class that they said they fancied filming me at. It was product development, a general major that just gave the students some broader information about life in fashion design. No dynamic flashes of coloured fabric, no intricate pieces of leatherwork, just a lecture and some note-taking. I said yes, of course, telling myself it might be my screen presence after all.

'They're following me to school!' I told my mom breathlessly the day before filming. I totally felt like I was the star of the show.

What an idiot.

Before long, I was waiting in a corridor at college being told I could head into my lecture shortly. There were no extras in *The Hills*. As with the scenes in clubs, nothing was closed or didn't run as normal, just because they were filming. The other students in my class filed into the room while I waited, hoping I wouldn't be too late. After a minute or two, the producers said it was okay for me to enter. In my naivety, I had assumed it was something to do with the lighting that had held me back, and as the door swung closed behind me I still didn't really think otherwise.

But as I walked to the one remaining desk and saw who was in my class, I realised that the producers had spotted something I had never known: one of my fellow pupils was my new nemesis, Lauren Conrad.

The register had been done already, so there was no doubt that Lauren would have known who I was. I saw her eyes widen as she noticed my entrance, and my cheeks burned red-hot beneath my make-up as I walked to my desk and tried to concentrate on the class we were being given. I was beyond shocked to see her. I knew she had studied at FIDM when *The Hills* had first started but it was the beginning of a new quarter, I had no idea she was even going to continue her studies there while she had an internship at *Teen Vogue*! Fashion was such a crucial part of her life – and of *The Hills* – but I was surprised that she was still taking her actual studies so seriously.

I was stuck, though. The cameras were rolling and the best I could do was to try and focus and get something out of the class. But it was nearly impossible! I had screamed at her only three nights earlier, thinking I might never have to see her again. I thought my part in *The Hills* would be to hang out with Heidi more, not be stuck with this Lauren girl.

If I only had known then what I know now. Because Lauren is just so nice. One of the best, most funny, honest and kind people who has ever been in my life. And she has since told me that she was actually a bit scared of me when I walked past her on that day. After all, I had been a firecracker of rage the last time she had seen me – she had no reason to suspect that I might have been a good person, just one seeing things from an entirely different perspective.

Once class was over my heart rate had just about calmed down again, and I decided there was really only one way to get to the end of term without a major incident: I had to apologise. So the minute there was a chance, I went over to her and said how sorry I was for what had happened at Opera. She seemed fine and we snuck off to the Zen Zoo Tea restaurant near the campus.

'Heidi has just been so upset,' I explained, hoping she would be able to see things from my point of view. Maybe I could even be the peacemaker?

'Things are a lot more complicated than that, though,' she replied. And I had no choice but to respect that and to try and find out what was really going on.

Lauren and I started a friendship that day, and it's one that continues to today. From the minute we sat down to chat in that café, I would hear her side of things as well as my brother's wherever Heidi was concerned. Since then I've got to know my brother better, and I realise more and more that there are always going to be people who don't get along with him or his way of doing things. Sometimes he deserves it, and sometimes he just comes across people who have made their mind up about him long before meeting him because of things he has said or done in the media. And I realise that I need to separate myself from taking sides, because I love my brother, but it's also perfectly possible to be a great person who just doesn't get along with him. Lauren was the best example of this – a wonderful woman who just didn't have time for Spencer. I could love both at the same time.

It was never going to be plain sailing, though. From the

very beginning I knew that I couldn't tell Spencer and Heidi that I was having these tea dates with Lauren after class, as they would probably want to kill me. So began a circle of lies. I would ask the crew on the show not to tell anyone that they had seen Lauren and me together after class, and before long we were basically having a secret friendship.

At the root of this new friendship was potential conflict, and although I was naive and optimistic enough to think that things would sort themselves out, it was this tension that kept the viewers' attention. Soon I was in more and more scenes, and the *The Hills* lifestyle was truly starting to become mine. The only negative was that I continued to feel as if I were flogging a dead horse with Heidi and Lauren, trying to persuade each of them to drop old resentments and move forward as friends again.

I'll tell you what makes flogging a dead horse a bit easier, though: a pay cheque from one of the biggest shows in the world, and the shopportunities that go with it. And I won't lie, those things were great. It wasn't just the salary that made me feel good, though: it was the contract itself.

I had made so many screw-ups in the years before *The Hills* came into our lives. I had let my family down, let my friends down, I had caused worry and hassle and unnecessary stress to so many people. So after those few trial scenes had aired and the producers said that they would like me to be on contract, to be a regular part of the show, I felt a rush of validation. I was finally doing well at something! Just the simple tasks of having to negotiate the fee, hire a lawyer and sort out the contracts gave me a confidence I hadn't had for years. It felt as if I were being taken seriously.

The attraction of *The Hills* was not to do with fame at this point. I didn't even really understand what that would be, or how it would manifest itself in my life, as opposed to Spencer and Heidi who were part of a couple. For me, it was to do with the feeling of having people need me, to do with earning my own money in my own way. I had always had my parents' credit cards and known that I could use them if there was something that I really wanted, but earning money, and having it go into my own account, was a totally different situation. I was independent after years of needing other people. Now I was part of something that needed me.

And I can't hide it, the money was great. For example, the week that I turned twenty-two I was able to go to Footcandy boutique in Brentwood, where they only carry the most exclusive designer shoes – and nothing else – and buy myself my first pair of serious designer shoes. Louboutins. It was crazy. You shouldn't be able to do that at that age unless you're some kind of prodigy! The moment I realised that that kind of thing was within my reach was huge.

It wasn't one hundred per cent pleasurable, though. The minute I stepped one of my Converse-clad feet over the doorway, I realised I was going to feel nervous the entire time that I was in there. I didn't really look like the average Louboutin customer, in my jeans shorts, my sneakers and my sporty sweatshirt. I knew that the sales person didn't believe I could be a serious shopper. He was a French guy with very manicured eyebrows, one of which he raised in what was a barely disguised sneer on seeing me. Yup, I was getting the look. You know, 'the look'. The 'Oh, you're just a child and you want to tell your friends you've been into the Louboutin store' look. Yeah, the 'I'd better keep an eye on you, you could drop a coffee or smear chocolate everywhere' look. The 'Meh, she can't wear these shoes, she'd snap a heel off' look. People can be so mean!

Instead of really wallowing in the moment of my first proper luxurious purchase, I just tried to get in and out of the store as fast as I could. I slightly didn't have faith that my card would work, anyway. But I bought the shoes and then left them in the trunk of my car for about a week. I can't believe they didn't see the light of day for so long, as they're so beautiful! Instead of the classic Louboutin black or red patent leather, they were in a fine pink and white striped fabric, a kind of candy striper look. It was slightly ruched all over, so from a distance they looked almost like pale pink snakeskin, and they were peep-toe and sling-back. Gorgeous as they were, I was too scared to take them home. I think it was because I didn't want my mom to know what I had spent. My parents have always been really generous with me, but they are also quite old-fashioned. There is no way my mom could have understood the idea of paying $1,000 for a pair of shoes. To her, that is bordering on immoral. She is a different generation and she just thinks there is no way that is what shoes cost.

I only wore those Louboutins once in the end, to the Season 4 wrap party. By that time, I did not feel guilty about shopping any more, and anything I did buy didn't stay in my trunk any longer. There was so much shopping that some stuff never got worn at all! The speed with which things moved once I was part of the show was breathtaking. It wasn't that I felt famous straight away; it was more like the big red curtain to the celebrity world had suddenly been pulled aside to let me in. I was on the other side of the velvet rope.

The first big event that I was invited to was the *US Weekly* Hot Hollywood 2008 party. I was beyond excited, as because of Spencer and Heidi's involvement and my time out in the clubs of LA, I had been close to this world for some time, but never yet been one of the VIP guests. In preparation I went to Betsey Johnson and got myself a black and white polka dot dress. To this day it is still one of my favourites, hanging in my closet in LA. I accessorised it with pearl earrings and had my hair done in curls again. By this time, things were worse than ever with Spencer and Lauren, and as I knew Lauren would be there, I was nervous that tempers would flare again. I chatted to my mom about it beforehand and her words of advice were simple. 'Whatever you do, be polite, and if you see Lauren there, just try not to be photographed with her – even if you do talk to her.' It couldn't be that hard, could it?

Well, it could if Lauren was the one I was meeting there. She was going with Lo Bosworth, her old friend from *Laguna Beach* who had also recently joined *The Hills*, and I was going with my friend Alishea. We pulled up in our car and didn't know anyone else there, so we just waited in the car until I had a message from Lauren that she and Lo were nearly there. We saw them arrive: they crawled up to the valet parking in a huge blacked-out Escalade, all big rims and tinted windows. I drew my breath and said to Alishea, 'Okay. This is the real deal.'

It was. This really was cool Hollywood. No cheesy limos or creepy old guys, it was just like *US Magazine* come to life! We got out and greeted each other, gave each others' outfits a quick look and did a lipstick check all round, then headed to the red carpet . . . my first red carpet. The thing about the red carpet at celebrity events is that it's very rarely the plush red carpet with a velvet rope each side that people imagine. In fact, the most important part is what the industry calls the 'step and repeat'. The step and repeat is a board with the title of the event and its sponsors printed all over it that you are all asked – well, encouraged – to stand in front of. That way, no matter what you do, who you kiss or how you fall, for the rest of time those photos will be tied to that event, promoting it forever and ever.

The thing is, I didn't know that then. I just saw cameras and panicked. And what had the cameras seen? The three girls from *The Hills*. All together.

'Girls! Lauren! Lo! Stephanie!' the paparazzi shouted at us. 'One of you all together!' The giant mass of camera flashes turned almost as one towards us, as the faceless men behind them carried on shouting instructions, encouraging us to stand closer together, to put our arms around each other, to smile and pose as one.

I had not even been there five minutes and already I was thinking, 'Oh GOD, this is the exact situation my mom told me to avoid!' But you can't get away from the step and repeat once you're in front of it. There is really no other way to access the party venue itself without finishing your walk past the board. And there is no way to get off the red carpet by going backwards because then you run the risk of two things: a set of photos of you trying to avoid the people you're with, turning your back on them and walking away, or a set of photos of you barging through the people behind you on the red carpet. For a first-timer, neither of these were ideal outcomes, so I decided to just stick with the first half of my mom's advice: be polite. The rest I could deal with tomorrow.

Once I was inside, it suddenly became much easier to forget about any problems that might be mounting up for tomorrow. The event was at Beso, Eva Longoria from *Desperate Housewives'* restaurant. It was gorgeous, a huge space with a nightclub attached. Brody was in there, and a few other friends I had made since joining *The Hills*. We were walked down to our own table in the VIP section by someone doing the kind of job that Heidi then was doing at Bolthouse PR. The area was roped off, just for us, with bottle service and food brought to us. There were photographers in the venue, but only ones approved by the event. On the tables there were branded drinks, and bowls and displays of free products – all sorts of things from hairstyling tools to jewellery. From time to time PRs and photographers would come up to us and ask if we would pose for an image with something from the table. At first, remembering my mom's words I was keen to be polite and simply answered, 'Of course!' before holding something up and smiling. The girls soon set me straight. It turned out we could get paid for those images, as they were so valuable to promote products, so I should never say yes and do it for free.

That party was the first of so many events that I went to while on *The Hills*, and there was always a huge variety in how fun – or not – they would be. Initially I was still so worried about doing something wrong, or getting in trouble, somehow letting someone down or causing another fight, but it was made easier by the fact that we were in all the best restaurants, having totally free nights and being treated like superstars – and being allowed, encouraged even, to do it with our best friends.

It turns out that 'young Hollywood' is really very small, and during the years I was on *The Hills* I started seeing the same people all the time. Often you would start a relationship with just a nod or a smile on the step and repeat, then there would be a 'hey' as you passed each other in the restroom then next time, then before long you'd be chatting as if you'd known each other forever, despite never actually having been introduced. At that time it was the cast of *The Vampire Diaries*, *Gossip Girl* or other reality stars like Kelly Osbourne at these parties. They also all had their own siblings and friends and make-up artists or whoever with them, making up their tables. So half the time you would recognise someone's face but they wouldn't be famous at all. You'd be thinking, 'Oh shit, are you from *The Vampire Diaries* or what?' and they'd just be someone's baby brother, but it was the third time you'd seen them that week.

For the first year or so, my level of fame was just right. The people who needed to know, knew who I was. I was getting fun invitations from the right places, but I wasn't getting any hassle or hatred from everyday people on the street. In a lot of ways, this period was spent like many people's college years are spent. A lot of partying, a lot of fun, and a lot of important friendships being built. People like Heidi, Lo and even people I met through them like my friend Simon Huck were all folk that have stayed friends for life and are still very much a part of my social world – whatever country I'm in. We would go out and party and then have a huge panic when we realised it was soon going to be time to leave the club. Me and Audrina or Lo or whoever would rush to the bathroom and be helping each other out with hair, powder and lipstick before having to face anyone who might be waiting outside. You know the deal, trying to realign a hairstyle that's been knocked about from too much dancing, or reapplying lipstick that was long left on endless champagne glasses. Girls all over the world are heading to the restroom in pairs for pep talks and a quick restyle, but in our case the results had the potential to make the national and international press. Sometimes we would try and find out if there were paps out there before we left, but sometimes we'd get it wrong anyway. There are just some nights that no matter how many sparkling eye drops you apply and no matter how great your lip liner looks, you still fall flat on your face when blinded by ten paparazzi hoping for a shot up your skirt.

Most of the time, we would be able to make it out with our dignity intact, holding on to each other, giggling and making fun of the ridiculous situation. Then, we would wake up the next morning, reach for our laptops and our Blackberries and check what the hell the online press had made of our night-time antics. In previous years celebrities would have to wait for the next day's papers, or for the weekly magazines, to print gossip about what we'd been up to. But the summer of 2007 was when the gossip websites really took off in earnest and by 2008 it was fever pitch. D Listed, Just Jared, X17 Online, Hollywood Gossip and Perez Hilton were all making a fortune from buying paparazzi pictures of us and putting up the story of what we'd been up to in a matter of hours. No more editors, picture editors or magazine layouts to worry about. Just a guy in a bedroom with a Wi-Fi connection. In Perez Hilton's case he didn't even have a Wi-Fi connection but started out working from the Coffee Bean & Tea Leaf café in West Hollywood. The gossip game had changed, and we turned out to be major players. The summer of 2008 seemed like non-stop fun, but we could never have imagined the long-term effects it would have on any of us.

The morning after the Hot Hollywood party Spencer and Heidi saw the photographs of us girls all together, and of course all hell broke loose. It was horrible to hear their anger and pain at what they felt was a betrayal, but I just about – just about! – managed to explain to them how I felt and how I had to follow my own path, make my own friendships and take my own opportunities.

Because by now, for the first time in my life, I was starting to feel as if I had a little bit of authority. The team at *The Hills* were pleased with how I was doing, and I had gone from having no confidence at all about myself to gathering a bit of self-respect. When I left rehab, I really did feel worthless after what I had put everyone who cared about me through. When you have had a serious addiction problem, you can often have wasted years of your life just by doing drugs. The only relationship I had known with people for so long was one of them being disappointed either in me or for me. I had wanted to prove myself to people but no one had trusted me to do anything – so how could I prove what I could do?

So after a few episodes, *The Hills* started to give me not just new friends, but structure in my life. I realised that I was part of making a good TV show, and as such I had to be where I said I was going to be when I said I was going be there. I couldn't let people down any more, and I liked the weight and seriousness that my contract represented. It was basically a huge media company saying, 'We need to rely on you to be part of this,' and that was a huge deal to a girl who had not really proved herself to be trustworthy in the past. The legal obligation I had to them was one of the cherished things in my life at that point – not because of the celebrity, but because of the responsibility. Having a job and a series of commitments – that I was meeting! – was slowly rebuilding my self-esteem.

Another big step in growing up on film was hiring a publicist. And then there were the perks that come with that . . . I had been on about four episodes when the mail started arriving for me. I kept my parents' address as my mailing address for the show at first, as Spencer and Heidi had done. After all, my new apartment – the first place I had bought, as soon as my money from the show started to come in – was only round the corner from them and I was still seeing them almost every day anyway. I had got used to the stacks of post – mostly clothes, bags and cosmetics – arriving for Heidi. My mom would stack it up for her and once every week or so when they were over, she would collect it. Then, after about a month, the packages started arriving for me.

I'll never forget the first time I was seen as worthy of being sent these gifts. I squealed, took everything home, unfolded it carefully, laid it all out on my bed, and then hung it all up in the right places in my cupboards. Once it began, the stream of packages seemed never-ending, though. It was everything from bikinis to jackets to jewellery. There would be a range from high street to high fashion, with names like Wildfox, Gypsy05 and Stila all regulars. But soon I couldn't keep up, and before long I would just select one or two pieces and give the rest to my housekeeper, or to charity.

Soon, I was being paid to wear different products, too. Frequently we would get emails from different PRs for brands, sending us a lookbook of ideas for different outfits. They would ask if we would wear them to this event or that, and we'd often be told that not only were the clothes gifted but that we would be paid $1,000 for wearing them. Yup, paid to wear free stuff. It seemed ridiculously lucky. I would tell my publicist what I wanted to wear, the clothes would turn up, and then later so would a payment.

Not long after the packages started arriving, *US Weekly* wanted to do a photo shoot with me, introducing me as one of the new characters in the show. I was thrilled when it ran in the magazine, and cut the photos out and taped them to my wall. Finally, I had a bit more respect and independence from my parents than I had ever had before.

I felt stronger and stronger with every passing week, especially as I was just about managing not to cause a stir when I went out in public. In my early days on the show, I had occasionally gone out for coffee with Heidi and heard people muttering that it was 'her from *The Hills*', but I always knew that it was Heidi they were referring to. In time, as Heidi's profile grew, we'd hear people calling her name. Then, over the course of that year, I'd start to hear the whispers of 'Heidi and Stephanie' in the street.

It takes a while to get used to total strangers recognising you in the street, though, especially if you've spent a few years out of it on drugs, not quite remembering names or faces, like I had. I had grown up in Los Angeles, around celebrities all my life, so I was taken aback to find myself one of them. At first when I heard my name I would assume

I was in trouble for something and immediately divert to thinking, 'What have I done now?!'

For months I would panic when someone approached me and said, 'Are you Stephanie?' It wasn't that I didn't want to talk or to sign something for them, but that I would assume they recognised me from rehab and I couldn't remember which one. I would say, 'Ye-es,' slowly, while my brain was whizzing with the thought, 'which rehab which rehab which rehab?' until eventually – if I was lucky – they would say that they liked my appearance in the show. I can only hope that they assumed the blank look on my face as I paused before talking to them was all part of a celebrity mystique!

Heidi's fame was always larger, though. People would start shrieking and following her down the street. I was always happier being a rung below on the fame ladder. It didn't take me long to observe that the way that reality TV works is that there can only ever be one 'alpha' female in the show. There's never more than one 'good' girl allowed. The boys – oh the boys can largely get up to whatever they want – but the rest of the girls usually have to be known for scandal or take a back seat. I was happy to be a satellite, famous as 'Spencer's little sister'. I was still not really strong enough to take the attention that they had. They were on the covers of magazines every single week, but always accompanied by controversy. There were as many people that didn't like them as did, and I knew early on that I was very far from being able to handle that, but at that point Spencer and Heidi seemed to be able to handle absolutely any criticism.

As much as Heidi could handle criticism from strangers, what she really wanted was her best friend back. And I wanted that for her, too. As time went on, my role in the show developed into being a sort of negotiator between Heidi and Lauren. It was a good feeling that for the first time I was trying to create peace, instead of making trouble, but I really had my work cut out with those two.

The dispute seemed to stem back to the fact that Lauren was never sure who had spread rumours that there was a sex tape showing her years before. This situation never really got resolved – Brody blamed Spencer, Heidi defended Spencer, Spencer pretended that he had done it – presumably just to play devil's advocate – but then later swore blind he didn't. And I for one believe him. He has his faults but he's not a sleazy guy. For months, it seemed as if whoever was prepared to even mention the damn sex tape immediately had the finger of guilt pointed at them. I'm not going to rake over old ground, because if some guy was out there trying to sell a sex tape he obviously didn't get very far! So, it was either rumours (and rumours that we should all have left well alone) or the person who had this tape was someone so disliked and untrustworthy that no news outlet would take it. But it was hard to let this lie with tabloids, websites, TV producers and even our own parents wanting to either fight their own side or get their own story.

With all my heart I wanted the girls to become proper friends again. I loved them both so much, I wanted there to be harmony in their lives, and I was sure for so long that I could change their minds. They really had been the very best of friends. Now that so many years have passed, not everyone remembers the first series of *The Hills*. It was originally a show about them, and their friendship! Trying to encourage them to rebuild that became exhausting, but it was also the main thrust of the show: the fighting between the two of them – originally about the sex tape, but then about Spencer's increasing role in Heidi's life. Every time I would see Heidi – on camera or off – she would be asking me about how things were with Lauren. Then every time I would see Lauren there would be a portion of the conversation that remained the same: 'Okay . . . you know what I'm going to say now,' before I launched into trying to persuade her to give the relationship another chance.' Yes,' she'd say, looking sad and tired. 'You know, you, and Heidi . . .' I'd give it another go, knowing it would never be worth it. And so on.

As time passed I started to feel bad around everyone, and the negativity spread to our family with Spencer becoming increasingly furious that I still dared to be friends with Lauren and her 'allies'. With Lauren, I could tell I was starting to annoy her. And around Spencer I felt bad that I had, as he saw it at that time, been dancing with the family enemy. The rage that he had then about me hanging out with Lauren was very real, so spending time with her – even when I was trying to help – often just felt as if I was storing up trouble that could explode in front of my parents, or worse, on screen.

That nagging anxiety about how things were affecting my parents began to mount up, and family tension – after we had all put in so much hard work following rehab – started to build up. It breaks my heart even to remember these times, as things are so very different now. But back then, the tension began to dominate. I started buying my mom amazing and increasingly lavish gifts for her birthday, or for Christmas, or just because she was sad. She would be worried about my brother and me so I would just pop out and get her a Balenciaga or a Chanel bag. 'Cheer up!' I'd say, as I presented it to her, hoping that that would mend things. Things had moved very fast from my first pair of Louboutins to buying a Chanel handbag just being the way that Heidi and I would finish off a lunch date. In 2008 my motto was, 'If money can't buy you happiness, then you're not spending your money on the right things.' But how long could I live by that?

8

By the end of 2008 it seemed that the white heat of the public's relentless attention might be getting to Heidi and Spencer after all. That November, they eloped to Mexico and had the first of their weddings. It wasn't legally binding, but the fact that they had headed out there without letting producers know until the very last minute was the first sign that perhaps being the tabloids' punch-bag might not be as much fun as they were making out.

We all knew that Heidi still wanted a 'proper' wedding though. In hindsight, I think she headed to Mexico on a whim under pressure – from the press, from Spencer, from everything – so I'm really proud of having helped to persuade them not to just formalise the wedding in the

LA courts but to go for a big traditional wedding – and go large they did!

In the spring of 2009 things between Spencer and I were so much happier, and he seemed to accept that my friend-ships with the girls from *The Hills* were not an act of specific aggression or disloyalty towards him. Even Lauren and Heidi had sort of formalised their distance from each other in a well-meaning way. Lauren made it clear that she would never not love Heidi, but that she still didn't trust Spencer.

Lauren and Spencer's relationship remained irretrievable, though, even if there was a whisper of hope for Lauren and Heidi's. Consequently, when the time came for the couple's 'real' wedding, I was pretty sure that Lauren would be a no-show. She had already decided to leave *The Hills*, which was a pretty big deal given that it was 'her' show, originally both about and narrated by her. And on top of that she had told me, my family, Spencer and Heidi, and the show, that she wouldn't attend the service. So even though I put on a brave face for Heidi's sake, still desperately hoping that there might be a tiny remaining chance for reconciliation, deep down I was convinced there would be no Lauren in the church that day.

The day itself was looking like it was going to attract a record-breaking amount of attention for Heidi and Spencer. And what a day it was. It looked fantastic, Heidi and Spencer were fabulously happy, and I really remember it as the high point of my time on *The Hills*, too. I was glowing with joy that the event was happening at all, and especially that it had all come about at a point when we were so close as a family, after the worst of the me-Lauren-Spencer fighting. Often wedding preparations end up being a stressful time for a family but for us, it was relative bliss! Holly, Heidi's sister, and I were to be bridesmaids and we had the most gorgeous bright yellow BCBG dresses. It was a spring wedding and the weather was just perfect, so the daffodil brights felt like wearing a smile! Heidi herself really did look like the fantasy princess that she had always dreamed she would. Her dress was a classic Monique Lhuillier, with a tight-fitting top and then a dreamy full-length skirt made up of layers and layers of ruffles. She was dripping in diamonds as only she could carry off, and went big on a train too, with it trailing all the way down her back. Her hair and make-up were perfect, and above all, she looked relaxed and happy.

You may have guessed it, but no, it wasn't all plain sailing on the day, though. The event was huge, bigger than even any of us had allowed for. The paparazzi were crawling around the whole area where the church was. It was insane as it's really just a sunny residential area, not the kind of place geared up for paparazzi. But there were hundreds, as far as the eye could see, when we approached the church, and of course when we left it after the ceremony. People were even camped out overnight, and sitting on roofs of nearby houses to try and get that perfect view or big-money shot. I have spent a fair few years at celebrity events now, but I have never, ever seen anything like the clamour that was there that day.

One contributing factor to the throng was that the cere-mony itself was delayed because the power went out in the entire building. We were all in the reception area in the basement, waiting for the service to begin. Heidi and I were talking with Holly and her mom when suddenly 'pfffft', then darkness. The volume of electricity being used for all the lighting and cameras – and possibly also the hairdryers downstairs – seemed to overload the system, and it was quite a while before things were up and running again.

No one wants to have a last-minute panic like that on their big day, but Heidi actually took it incredibly well – especially as we'd been discussing pre-wedding jitters just as it happened. It was such a stressful position to be in, exacerbated by knowing that there were all those crowds outside wondering what was going on. I'm quite sure people assumed there had been a terrible hitch in the relationship, not just that the cameras and lights had knocked everything out. They must have been imagining fireworks, while the reality was that us girls were sitting in the basement snacking and chatting like our lives depended on it. And thanks to fate and the electrics, this meant that Lauren made it after all.

It was the icing on the cake for Heidi that she managed to have that little chat with her one-time BFF before heading up the aisle. I had been hassling them to be friends again for so long by this point, that I felt almost as relieved as Heidi. It was wonderful that Lauren came to show support for her old friend, and I know that it meant that when the wedding march finally did start (three hours late!) Heidi really was living the dream.

As we stood on the steps of the church that afternoon I don't think I could have been happier either. It felt as if so many tensions had been lifted from all of us. Both of the couple's families were there, smiling and wishing them well. We had resolved everything and I thought that the madness of previous years was over at last. We were so close, and so were they – all fallings-out resolved. Little did I know that it would be the last fond memory I would have of them for some time.

Not long after the wedding the couple started to become increasingly isolated. As they were now married, they were doing things like looking for a family home together, and going out less than ever before. The show reflected this, too – they were very rarely with the rest of us unless it was a big group event. They were also hugely in love (and still are!), so spending a lot of time together didn't seem that unusual to any of us. If anything, we respected it, particularly because of the success of the wedding. And as Lauren had left the show and was spending more time with friends and on fresh work projects elsewhere, I was sure that things would settle down soon.

Consequently, none of us were unduly worried when Spencer and Heidi were not able to spend Thanksgiving with us that year, or Christmas. We were hearing from them less and less, but we wanted to be respectful and keep out of their way. They were busy with promotional appearances a lot of the time, but also they were hardly the first couple to want to spend their first married holidays together and alone. I thought it was actually kind of romantic, and sad though we were, no one was worried. Yeah, we wanted to hang out with them and bask in the reflected happiness of the newly-weds, but even my mom understood that we couldn't bother them while they were spending special time together.

What we didn't realise was that they were keeping a secret from absolutely every single one of us. In early January 2010, two months since any of us had seen them, my mom drove her shopping cart past the magazine rack at Gelson's and saw Heidi's face smiling back at her from the cover of *People* magazine. But it wasn't quite the same face. The secret was out.

As has now been really, really well documented in the press, Heidi had had ten cosmetic surgery procedures – in one day – and had made an agreement with *People* magazine to keep the whole thing secret until the interview with her was on the shelves. I don't know what made Heidi have that much done. None of us can ever really understand what goes on in someone else's mind. But it was her business, not any of ours. I don't want to judge Heidi for her decision, particularly as she is a woman more beautiful on the inside than most of us could ever hope to be, but it is fair to say we were all pretty shocked.

We were also massively concerned when we found out what they had been through. Suddenly it made sense why the couple had been so quiet for so long. But it wasn't just that they were trying to keep the surgery a secret; there was also the fact that Heidi nearly died because the painkillers she was given had slowed her breathing down and it almost stopped. It was only in the week that followed that we discovered the full horror of what they had been through. At a time when Spencer was continuing to take an ongoing hammering in the press worldwide, he had been nursing his new wife back to health, entirely alone. A lot of the press coverage suggested that he had put pressure on her to have that amount of surgery done, but that simply wasn't the case. He supported her every decision because he loves her. The criticism at such a delicate time was just pressure upon pressure.

We soon found out what an incredibly draining and lonely time it had been for both of them, and as a family we were so sad that we hadn't been able to be there for him – or her! My parents are not judgmental people; they would have done absolutely whatever they could to help.

Spencer had been very isolated while caring for someone who had literally been wrapped up like a mummy. There was emotional isolation and there was also physical isolation. Physically, Heidi could not really be around people. She couldn't hug them. No one could really touch her. You can still see how delicate she was in the online videos that accompanied the *People* magazine piece.

The love of his life had almost died, heaping an intense level of responsibility on to Spencer. It must have been such a complicated set of emotions to deal with, made only more acute by the secrecy. Both of them were seeing their faces online, on TV and on the front of almost every magazine week in, week out. It was a level of scrutiny only comparable to that which the Kardashians have now . . . but there are more of them to share the burden! There were a solid two or three years of their lives where this was the situation every single week, and no matter how much love they had between them, it could not help but take its toll.

It breaks my heart to recount it, but this was the beginning of such a sad period for Heidi and Spencer, and I wish I had been able to understand it better and navigate it with more empathy back then. Aaaah, hindsight! Gradually, they seemed to fall out with everyone and seemed to be at a place where they decided that everyone was talking shit about them regardless of what they did.

They believed the whispers would never end, so made

the decision, 'We don't need your approval, we're going to do what the hell we want.' And that was when they seemed to start operating as if from their own little island. There was so much pain around the couple that they could have turned in many directions at this point. Everyone has their own path in life but, well, I don't think it's unfair to say that their choice of crystals as a way out was a little unusual. I'm not one to judge – after all, I have made my mistakes in what I've turned to for solace!

No one could have predicted that the next phase in the Heidi and Spencer story would be spending a fortune on healing crystals. I'm not even sure how it started, but all of a sudden they were spending up to $50,000 on various crystals to provide them with healing energy to try and keep the vibes around them positive. I don't even know where you would get a $50,000 crystal, but I do know that they had them – and they had a lot. Spencer has even said that they spent $500,000 on them. They still have them today!

They were dealing with healers who told them that because everyone was talking crap about them wherever they went, it was unleashing backchat on them. They told them they didn't need to deal with all this bullshit all day every day. And they were right – Heidi and Spencer did not have to take it. Heidi's face and body were hers and hers alone to do what she wanted with, and no one had the right to call her the things that people were calling her by then. But crystals probably weren't the way out. They treated them kind of like people use evil eye necklaces, to ward the haters away. They had jewellery with crystals on, they carried them loose, the works . . .

The saving grace is that they were really, really funny about it for a long time. They knew other people thought it was silly but they were determined to go with it. Heidi would let you play with her crystal wand, or bless you if you fancied it. There's always someone with a new crazy fad in Hollywood, and most of them aren't prepared to have a bit of a giggle about it, so for a while it all seemed pretty harmless if it was cheering them up.

But the energy that they ended up putting into their crystal collection and realigning of good vibes meant that they weren't as interested in the drama required to make *The Hills* the show it by now was. They knew they couldn't be wallflowers on screen as their roles were as key instigators of so much of the action. They used the crystals to keep a sort of distance between them and the rest of the world. And it was this distance that seemed to be the end of their time on *The Hills* and to cause some temporary disruption in our relationship. This was one of the hardest times for our family, and certainly one of the worst periods of my time on the show. We didn't know what to do, how to close the distance they were keeping from us. They were only down the road but it felt like miles away. I can remember driving down the freeway one morning and hearing Ryan Seacrest on his show talking about what they were up to now and I had to pull over until I had stopped crying: Ryan Seacrest is a nice guy but he's not who should be telling you what your family is up to. Even thinking about those times now makes me horribly sad.

By now, people were saying all sorts of things about them, and even I never really got to the bottom of what the definitive reason they left *The Hills* was. Pragmatically speaking, I suppose their role in a show that was largely about who was dating who was unsustainable once they had been married over a year, and it was best for everyone when their appearances on it ended. It's a period best left forgotten for everyone. Looking back on it now, it doesn't really matter anyway, as what came next was one of the happiest periods of their lives.

I was still in LA, missing my pal Lauren and wondering what to make of Kristin Cavallari making the show her own. She appeared as a replacement for Lauren, taking over the voiceover and role as the lead character. Meanwhile, Spencer and Heidi headed for Costa Rica, for what they called their spiritual cleansing. They had always wanted to spend time in Costa Rica, and long talked about a life away from Hollywood, without the worries and materialistic bullshit that had been dogging them. It had got to a point where they would go shopping and spend $50,000 in one store just to distract themselves, and that wasn't making them happy anyway. They wanted out. They needed to go back to basics, and that's exactly what they did.

They spent months out there, freed from the burden of looking camera-ready. Heidi's hair grew unkempt and Spencer's beard reached new levels of bushiness. It was a rebellion against the perfection they had fought to achieve. They stayed at the Four Seasons, and spent their days ordering room service then walking barefoot along the beaches with their dogs off the leash chasing the monkeys playing there. The way they talk about it now, it sounds like a dream. Truly, it was the escape that they needed.

They were there for about three or four months. We hadn't heard from them for so long that we thought the family might have lost them forever. But when Spencer called my dad about coming home, he didn't hesitate to extend the hand of forgiveness. My dad sorted their return trip, flying them by private jet into Burbank California as discreetly as he could and waiting for them on their arrival with the biggest hug ever. He drove them to our beach house in Santa Barbara and came home to my mom. The next day she called me and said, 'Spencer and Heidi are back. They are at the beach house.' I couldn't believe it, the family was reunited. The sigh of relief was enormous.

And since that return nearly five years ago they have really built a life they can be proud of. Last summer – ten years after he started it – Spencer completed his degree in Political Science at the University of Southern California.

They are happier, calmer and lovelier than ever. Sure we had our moments, and I'm not thrilled that the worst of it was caught on camera, but I can say with an open heart that that is behind us now, just as it was when they returned from Costa Rica.

By the time Heidi and Spencer were back, *The Hills* had finished, so the option for them to return to it was no longer there. It was the end of an era, but by that time, it was an era I was ready to say goodbye to.

9

Apart from the obvious sadness and stress that the situation with Spencer and Heidi created, there were other things that the show brought to my life that I was totally unprepared for. Some were, shall we say, better than others.

One of the less good was the way that Brody Jenner behaved towards me. We grew up together, he'd been like an older brother to me for years and years, but in Season 4 and Season 5 of the show, he started behaving like some sort of nemesis. I guess he just didn't like me being on the show. The whole thing of him and Spencer being 'the princes of Malibu' was theirs, and they had made the reality dream work after a false start, then I showed up and started getting as much air time as him. I guess that stung his ego.

I had been a little sister who could just be batted out of the way when she was annoying the boys . . . then all of a sudden that had changed. I was clean, I was in control of my life, and I was enjoying my new role. But there was no reason to be as cruel to me as he was, particularly where my past was concerned.

He stirred up a lot of trouble when Doug, Lauren's ex, asked me to go on a date, and I went. Even though I had texted Lauren about the date, and she had said it was okay, Brody dived right in with the telling tales and shit-stirring. But worst of all was what happened in Season 4 when we all went off to Las Vegas for the weekend for Brody's birthday. There was a bit of tension in the air from the outset with that trip. Alongside my own worries, it was a period when Audrina's growing relationship with Justin Bobby was harming her relationship with Lauren, and Lo to an extent. I knew something was up when we were on the jet there, and Brody made a sly comment about not trusting me as part of a toast. Then not long after we arrived, a bunch of us were eating together when suddenly Brody randomly called me a psycho when I asked him about why he thought Lauren shouldn't trust me. He'd been telling Lauren to keep away from me, and I wanted to know why. He seemed to be heavily implying that he knew something dreadful about me, and he brought up my past drug problems as if they were a reason for me to be disliked or made me a bad friend. It is the only time in the entire show that anyone mentioned it, and I was absolutely floored when he spoke to me like this. He seemed to be using something that had happened before I was even on *The Hills* as a reason to exclude me from the group, rather than finding anything in my recent behaviour.

I had never hidden what I'd been through – you don't get that option when you've been on the news for being arrested high in Hawaii – but it was in my past, not my present. I didn't really want that out there by then, being the focus of people's opinions. I was twenty-three, and I had been through so much. I had seized a chance at a fresh start and was having that thrown back in my face. Brody didn't have any reason beyond screen time not to want me around, so he found something from years ago to wield as a weapon.

What I really couldn't take was Brody drawing a parallel between drug abuse and being mean, a bad person or unworthy of a good friend's trust. Even when I was using, I wasn't a cruel person. Most addicts aren't cruel people. Lots of them do stupid stuff, often with horrible consequences. But having had an addiction doesn't mean you're a bitch forever. Almost everyone in my life had been supportive of my trying to get clean and stay clean, and even Brody himself had come to visit me in Clearview with his then girlfriend Nicole Richie. It had been almost impossible to get clean, with so many false starts, but I had done it. And instead of helping me, Brody was now doing just the opposite – he threw it in my face, publicly, as if

I were an alien. A friend – which I thought he was – should have celebrated my sobriety, not attacked it and left me feeling weaker.

One great thing came out of that moment in Vegas, though: a quote that so many girls remember to this day! Brody really did just throw his unkindness out there on camera, and my first instinct was just to get away from the table. I ran into the bathroom and was crying hysterically when Lauren found me. It was so out of the blue for someone to start attacking me like that, and for something that was no longer part of my life. I couldn't even catch my breath I was crying so hard, when Lauren came and took care of me.

'Don't cry over someone who wouldn't cry over you,' she told me. And thus one of the most used quotes from the whole series was born. It really was a gem of wisdom, in that moment and forever. Even today it is still used all of the time on Instagram and Pinterest, with girls quoting it to each other to help them through grim fights and broken hearts. I love it! For that alone, the grim trip to Vegas was almost worth it – it was one of the best moments of girl bonding I ever felt – and one that has lived on for others.

Another concern for me was that I had started off just as Spencer's sister, and then had acted as a sort of bridge between Lauren and Heidi as their split became deeper and sadder. This meant I was close to both camps – both

Lauren and the friends who felt that Spencer and Heidi had done her a disservice, and my brother and his now wife. I started to see that when the show aired, I seemed like something of an instigator. Increasingly, it looked as if I were the one making things happen – I egged Heidi on to go to Lauren's birthday party on the boat. I was just trying to make everyone happy! But by the time the show aired it was perfectly clear the plan was a disaster. Again and again, I was inviting people to places or encouraging them to talk – but what was me trying to create harmony often just resulted in chaos.

At the time, I didn't mind. I was twenty-three, I was part of a great show, and letting the world in on the action was just a part of me doing my job. But you can't live like that, when you don't know who's got your back, forever. Lauren knew this, and that is why she was so wise to leave when she did. Whitney, who had long been Lauren's friend in the show – they had been working together at *Teen Vogue*, and spending a lot of that time discussing my brother and his wife – was the same. As the conflict got worse, she wanted out, and she took the chance to leave when she could.

As the show progressed, it turned out that despite the confrontations and anxiety between all of us, what was really getting to me was what the rest of the world was saying about me – and how they were saying it. At first, I'd find out that my picture was going to be in a magazine and it would be really exciting. Maybe they would have done a shoot with some of us girls from the show, or maybe we'd find out that some press photos from an event we'd been to would be being used, and we'd hope that they were some of the good ones. Then, the magazine would come out in print, there were no reader comments, and if we didn't like the image or what was said about us, well . . . there'd be another issue out next week.

Then came the internet. When online showbiz websites and blogs started to sprout up, they changed the industry forever. The magazines had to play dirtier to keep up with the websites, and the websites seemed kind of lawless. Worst of all was when the website had a real sense of 'a voice'. And the worst for this was Perez Hilton. Because once the author of the blog has hit the tone for what they're saying about someone, the commenters will take their lead from this. So if Perez chose to write about you, you didn't just get whatever vile little bitchiness he had come up with, but you had thousands of his followers trying to mimic him below the article. Before long, it seemed as if these comments were all I was ever going to see, and that they'd go on forever.

It began in my first episode on the show, because of Lauren calling me the 'She-Pratt'. It was a funny nickname, and obviously I ended up becoming friends with her almost immediately, but that name stuck, and I hated it. I never really minded the 'prat' bit – hell, we'd all been dealing with that all our lives! What I hated was that it robbed me of my identity. It put me in the context of my brother not as a person in my own right. It makes me sound not human. It's just too close to 'She-monster'.

If only I had known that that would not be the worst of it. Over time, the way that bloggers – especially Perez Hilton – wrote about me got worse and worse. It wasn't just personal stuff, and it wasn't that it was not even true half the time, it was that it used really graphic violent imagery. About someone who was just in a show about going shopping and hanging out with your mates?

Then, once people had found my mugshot from my arrest in Hawaii, it was used almost every time I looked anything less than close to perfect. I have worked through any issues I have with that image, but it was horrific that my past drug use was used as a cheap joke again and again . . . and again. Just when I thought I'd had a fresh start, I was a 'meth-head' all over again.

Perez would use that nick-name for me loads, but the irony was I don't actually think he had a clue about my past meth use. He knew that something had been up when I was in Hawaii, of course. But he just seemed to slap the meth stuff around because it sounded cool when he felt like being vile. There was absolutely no regard for the fact that he was talking about a recovering addict.

To overcome an addiction is to put in a level of work into not taking drugs every single day. You have to choose not to be falling prey to temptation again and again, especially in those first few years. To effectively have someone throwing hammers at you makes that work hundreds of times more hard. It was indescribably discouraging. Over and over, I would have to stop myself from thinking, 'It doesn't matter what I do. All the months and years I have been sober count for nothing as I am still known as a meth-head. So what's the fucking point? I may as well just do it all again if you're still going to tar me with that brush.' That was the addiction talking and it talks much louder when you hear people like Perez attacking you so loudly and so directly.

Five years ago he wrote about me,

'Listening to Stephanie Pratt speak is like being stabbed repeatedly with thousands of FUG, meth-faced, tiny little knives. Listening to Stephanie Pratt speak about being slutty with various men is like pouring kerosene on the previously mentioned knives stabbing you, and then lighting a match.

BARF.'

Truly, it was beyond me. And back then this was a new phenomenon, so people just didn't know how long this would go on for, or how bad it would get. I didn't know to Just Not Read, like I do today. It was merciless, for years. I would be out having a great day, then I would get a text from my mom or my brother saying, 'Oh honey have you read this, are you okay?' and suddenly I would see an email containing the latest post. There would be photos with his 'trademark' doodles on them – either semen drops coming out of my mouth or cocaine dots drawn all around my nose. I didn't really speak to my mom about sexual stuff, and I hadn't had many boyfriends then because of all the time that had been sucked away by my drug problem. So to have those visuals as well as the blog itself calling me a whore so relentlessly was especially humiliating.

No one ever sent me links to this stuff out of malice; it was more about trying to make sure that I was okay, that I was coping. But the end result was the same. There was a constant drip, drip, drip of information out there – being read by millions – that I was little more than a meth-head. Anyone who knows anyone who has ever had a drug problem knows how unbelievably hard it is to get away from that label. It is so destructive. It is so discouraging. It continually makes the point that there is no use in changing, which is just about the worst thing you can let someone in that vulnerable position think about themselves.

But Mario Lavandeira – as Perez Hilton is actually called – particularly chipped and chipped away at me. He made a fortune out of his weird little obsessions with other people and his desperation to be a somebody himself. I was just someone on a reality TV show trying to manage an addiction. I wasn't harming anyone else, I wasn't bringing negativity to anyone else. I wasn't encouraging cruelty in anyone else. But he viciously threw those insults for years, regardless of any potential consequences – for myself or anyone else.

After all, *The Hills* was watched by young impressionable girls, it was featuring young impressionable girls, and Perez's blog was really popular with young impressionable girls. So it was creating a cycle of acceptability that if you put yourself out there on TV, you will be judged for things you haven't done or said on TV, and that is okay. And that even if you weren't doing meth and you weren't walking around with semen around your mouth people will put those associations on you anyway, just because you're a girl with a bit of celebrity. (After all, the guys never got it. Even when Spencer was taking heat in the media it was rarely for his appearance. For us, it was daily comments.) That created a circle of insecurity beyond me that showed the audience and young girls that it was okay to talk like this about us, and each other. Why should one unhappy man with a laptop have that power over a whole load of women? Could he not live his own life? Given his performance on this year's *Celebrity Big Brother*, it seems perhaps not . . .

Either way, the result was the same. I would go home after seeing some of the things that were being put out there about me, and especially my looks, and want to never leave the house again. I had overcome an addiction, but was still labelled a drug addict. I had done my job well on the show, and made good friends, but there was still this black cross through my name in the media.

So by early 2009 I did start staying in a bit more, just watching TV and ordering pizza. Increasingly, I knew that whatever invitation I got I would be happier at home eating. I just never felt good about myself any more, so going out felt less and less appealing. It wasn't like I waited until the last minute and bailed on parties before I was meant to be at them, I simply became a really big flake who didn't commit to anything.

During the day, I was finding it increasingly stressful to get ready when a crew was coming over to film anything with me. It was a nightmare. I would try on a million different outfits, unhappy and panicked about what people would say about each one. I lived by myself in that apartment, so I had no one to sound out outfit ideas on when I was getting ready and crucially, no one to tell me when things were getting a bit out of hand.

I knew that the camera adds ten pounds, so I would have that stressing me out. And I knew that I put on weight really fast, so I would be worrying about that too. With the logic that only someone with a depressive personality can apply, I figured, 'Well if I look fat in everything anyway, I may as well eat.' And eat I did . . .

Before long, the only way that I was able to cope with all of these feelings was by eating, specifically embracing the comfort of cheese. I would eat that a lot. So much.

Grilled cheese, cheese fries, pieces of cheese. The lot. Then, because I knew that I would be filming the next day with all the others, who were all so slim, I would have to get the cheese out. I became bulimic. Really fast.

It was totally mindless. I didn't know about all the chemical reactions that were going on because of me eating badly. When I was getting a sugar high from white carbohydrates or whatever I just thought, 'This is what I'm getting, because this is what I need.' It was largely take-out food that I was eating. I very rarely went shopping for my own ingredients. I was going to restaurants nearby where I had grown up, heading to little places in the Palisades that I'd gone to all my life. There were no people staring at me because I was famous, only locals who knew me for me. It was just like, 'Hey Steph, is this one yours?' as I waited at the desk for my order, not, 'OMG She-Pratt eats.'

It wasn't even just the food or the taste of the food that I seemed to be craving – it was eating what I used to eat when I was a child, when I was happier and more settled. I was ordering off kids' menus a lot – chicken tenders, grilled cheese, pizza, buttered pasta. I was retreating from what my life had become, to how I often now wished it had remained: staying at home to watch reruns of *Friends* and eat buttered pasta.

I was so unhappy with my weight that before long the throwing up became a regular, planned part of the pattern. I had to drink a lot of water to do it. I would fill a huge water bottle to make it a lot easier, then gulp it all down to sort of shock my stomach. Then the problem was that when you're throwing up, your eyes start to water and then I would start crying. It would be exhausting, so I would have to go and get into bed, and fall asleep to *Friends*.

I knew when the crew was coming over to film and I learned to time it all perfectly. I knew I wanted to get that 'special' meal in whenever I could. If I knew they were coming over mid-afternoon I'd know I needed my meal for twelve in order to have time to eat and get rid. But sometimes it didn't work, I couldn't get the food up, and I would keep the crew outside, saying, 'I am still getting ready!' But really I would be fixing my make-up to hide the crying, and washing repeatedly so that my hands didn't smell of sick any more.

It was the loneliest thing in the world. I was eating by myself and my mealtimes had become really long. I couldn't go out to eat what I wanted. And I was physically keeping people out of my house to get on with what I 'needed' to do.

I knew what I was doing. I knew it was bulimia. I just always thought it was going to be temporary. I never, ever thought I was going to live the rest of my life like this. But that's what I thought about drugs, and they would have killed me if something dramatic hadn't happened. It was a case of if I can get into this dress I'll stop, I'm just doing this 'til the end of the season. Next week I am sure everything will be back to normal. Once I feel better I'll stop doing this but right now I'm just doing it because I feel bad.

Same old, same old. This has always been a problem of mine. The need for instant gratification when I am in a time of anxiety. I always choose what seems like a great short-term solution, but is only ever going to rack up a whole load of long-term problems. Indeed, the next step seemed even crazier. I noticed that on screen and in pictures my face was starting to look bigger, even though my body was really small. I Googled 'effects of bulimia' and what do you know – it can give you a puffy face from all the purging. Of course being bent over the toilet throwing up pretty much every day isn't going to leave you looking great. I realised it had to stop.

I just stopped eating altogether.

'Great!' I thought. 'I have worked out how to cure my bulimia! I won't have to throw up if I don't eat it in the first place . . .'

Eating disorders are never that much about food, and often so much more about control, and creating emotional responses. The more I saw my image tugged and tossed about by other people – especially with such cruelty – the more I tried to somehow regain control over myself. But I was just making myself ill again.

By now *The Hills* was such a monster hit, and I was a key cast member, so I was busy enough that I was able to just get on with things while missing meals. I didn't have to plan my life around binges and keeping myself alone for ages like I had been. It seemed less lonely, but I'm not sure I was kidding anyone. I was drinking energy drinks, smoking, living so unhealthily. I was on a sugar and caffeine roller coaster that wasn't far from the old unhealthy habits I had been in a couple of years before.

I hate to think how things would have ended up if what happened next hadn't taken place. I guess I was lucky to have a huge stroke of bad luck. Fate intervened and I got the wake-up call I needed to take care of myself. In September 2009 I was arrested a second time. I know, it sounds crazy. And at the time I was distraught. But now I can see that this arrest came at exactly the right point to shock me back into respecting myself and my health.

The night it took place was Heidi's sister Holly's birthday party. The Empire in Hollywood was hosting the event and I went along with Holly's best friend Stacie, 'the bartender' – who had joined the show and our group of friends, and made a play for Spencer towards the end of his time in the show – her brother and a few others. I wasn't feeling great about myself that night, so I had – as I often did – offered to drive some of the others. As usual, I wasn't really drinking, and I certainly didn't have any of the endless shots or cock-tails that were being brought to our table. By this point I was barely over a hundred pounds, and I'm five foot seven tall. I should not have been drinking at all – there was nowhere for it to go. I had less than a whole glass of champagne the entire evening, but even that was too much for me. I had lost the ability to process alcohol at all.

We left the club late, around 3.00 am. I was with Stacie and her brother, and my agent Jennifer was in the car, too. At that time I had a very flashy car – a white BMW X5, with black 22-inch rims and tinted windows. Strictly speaking tinted windows are not legal in California, but a lot of people have them because of the dazzle of the sunlight. The reason you're not allowed them is because it means outsiders can't see in the car – which is exactly the reason lots of celebrities have them. Celebrities get pulled over for it the whole time. After they get pulled over they get them uninstalled, and then often just get them reinstalled a while later.

Like I say, the car was not discreet – it looked like a celebrity's car. We were driving home along Hollywood Boulevard and were stopped at the traffic lights outside of Eva Longoria's restaurant Beso, when out of nowhere a police car pulled up alongside me with its lights on and indicated that I should pull over. So I did, right there. It was not like being pulled over on a small residential street, it was the equivalent of being asked to do it in Knightsbridge or the King's Road in London.

'Do you know why I have pulled you over?' said the cop.

'No, I don't. I was waiting at the light.'

'It is because you have tinted windows.'

'Okay.' I wasn't sure what the penalty for this would be. I had had my window down as I was smoking a cigarette when he pulled me over, but there was no way I could hide or deny the state of the windows.

'Have you been drinking tonight?' he asked.

'No, I haven't,' I replied. As far as I was concerned, I hadn't been drinking. I had not even finished a whole drink! But I understood why he wanted to do this, so I got out of the car to do the roadside test. The cop really took his time with this, and it didn't take long for some of the photographers who regularly prowl that area to spot what was going on, notice the flashy car, and see the opportunity for some shots they could sell for decent money in the morning.

Stacie's brother, who was a cop himself, tried to talk to the guy who had pulled me over, and explain that I really hadn't been drinking. But he didn't care for the chat, and wanted to proceed with the breathalyser. I thought I had been being responsible by barely drinking a thing, but I was wrong. I took the test, and scored .08, which is bang on the legal limit. I thought I was fine until the officer explained to me that being on the limit is still illegal. In that moment I knew two things: I was in big trouble, and you really cannot drive with any alcohol in you. At all. Ever.

I started crying. A lot. Just sobbing. I was exhausted,

hungry, panicked, humiliated, and I really hadn't been trying to get away with anything I thought was wrong.

'Oh no, I can't get arrested again,' I cried.

And the minute those words left my lips I knew I had made things worse for myself. The cop's ears pricked at the word 'again', and immediately he took a firmer tone with me.

'I've come so far, I can't go back. What have I done wrong?'

But the more I cried the worse I made it. The cop made it clear that I was now going to be arrested for DUI and was being taken to jail. I was hysterical. My agent tried to reassure me, and said that she would take my car home for me. I left her with my purse and everything I knew I did not want in prison.

Before long I was in the drunk tank. It was the West Hollywood station, which didn't have segregated sections. To keep the women 'safe' they just handcuff them to a long bench. I was sitting next to several prostitutes who had been working to get their next fix. Around us there were guys sleeping in their own vomit. The floor was tiled, with drains in it to catch the fluids that were in plentiful supply. Around the drains there were cockroaches feasting on what they could.

Of course, there was a part of me that had got used to being pampered, earning good money and not having to deal with the nastier side of life, thinking, 'Ew, I do not belong here with my designer clothes and my professionally done hair and make-up.' But the bigger part of me was panicking: I had seen the dark side of life and the law before, and I had worked really hard to get away from it. I was surrounded by examples of what can happen if you let drink or drugs get the better of you, and I was terrified that I was on a path to destruction again.

Early in the morning I was moved to the Van Nuys jail in the Valley where my paperwork was processed. I remember staring out of the back window of the police car at about seven in the morning, seeing people driving to work and thinking, 'This is my life, in the back of a police car watching other people live their lives.'

The environment at Van Nuys was not really any better than in West Hollywood. The only difference was that the women were segregated into an area of their own. I was in a proper cell, filled with women, but the atmosphere was far from all girls together. There was a payphone in the cell, with a huge line to use it. I tried to keep my head down, hoping no one would recognise me. I didn't want to get into a fight with anyone. The phone conversations I heard in those few hours were incredible. They added to the sense of menace there, as I realised the compromised situations that so many of these women were in and who they had to call in their darkest hour. It was a world even I had never imagined.

I knew I didn't want to call my mom. I was still clinging to the hope that she wouldn't have to find out about this.

So I called my long-suffering agent, who said she would come and get me when they released me. Eventually, at around 11.00 am, I was free to go. But not entirely free: the story of my arrest had already made the online news, and the jail was crawling with paparazzi. The police said that I could leave out of the back, via the garage. Jennifer was there, waiting for me.

I was in last night's clubbing clothes and heels, now accessorised with streaked make-up and ratty hair. Jennifer drove me home, as I prayed my parents hadn't seen the news. All I could think about was how another arrest would destroy them, and the trust that we had built between ourselves after the years of drug abuse.

I walked in the front door, and the first thing I saw as I entered the living room was my mom crying on the sofa.

'It's not my fault! It's not what you think!' I blurted out. Depression engulfed me again and this time I wasn't numbed by drugs. But the tragedy was that they had heard it all before. Of course, they just assumed it was back to the old Steph. They – understandably – assumed I was back on drugs and that this was the direct result. They saw how thin I was, how unhappy and fragile I was and reached a pretty sensible conclusion. I was flaky, I was crying all the time, I was a wreck. I knew it wasn't drugs but I also knew I needed help. The Spencer and Heidi situation, the pressure of the press, the way that the show kept us in a constant state of conflict to get good ratings, the social isolation I had created for myself because of my eating habits. It was too much.

I really thought my life as I knew it was over at that point. I went upstairs to bed and stayed there for hours. The production team arrived at my parents' house wanting to film my reaction to the night's events for the show. The last thing I wanted or needed was to be filmed.

There was a massive wall between my parents and me because of everything that had happened in the past. But I was determined not to head back to square one. One thing I really learned in rehab was to acknowledge when you need help, and to tell someone instead of trying to keep up a brave face. At least I saw that I had reached that point, and thankfully had the courage to admit it. I really had only one option.

'I'll do whatever you think is best, and if that means going to rehab again, fine. I'll do whatever, anything.' I just wanted them to know and to trust me that I wanted to make it right. So I went to the Betty Ford Center. I spent two weeks as an outpatient there, commuting every morning from my nearby hotel. It didn't take them long to clock that my weight was a major issue, and I cracked immediately upon being asked. By the time I had left two weeks later I had a better understanding of how little alcohol it takes to be DUI. I had stopped smoking and I was eating properly again. In a way, that arrest saved me from going down another dark path.

I met my boyfriend Josh Hansen not long after leaving rehab, as the end of *The Hills* was on the horizon. By the time we filmed those final few episodes, I was ready to move on and get to work on some fresh projects. I was, of course, hoping that I would be doing it with Josh by my side, but as you know, that was never going to happen. After all, he clearly had one eye on life off camera, with all the pool party plans he was making . . .

The informal cast and crew wrap party for the show was an incredibly emotional event. In a way, it felt like the college graduation that I had never had. I wore a pink dress by Elizabeth and James and some Louboutins I adored, and I had my hair and make-up all done. But the minute I walked in the room I burst into tears at seeing everyone. *The Hills* had been such a huge part of my life – it had taken its toll at times but it had also played a massive role by turning my life around. It gave me opportunities I could never have dreamed of, and taught me an unbelievable amount.

Seeing all those faces again – from both sides of the camera – gathered together one last time really brought out the tears and soon my make-up was fighting for survival. We were all excited about the different projects we had lined up – Brody was going to be part of the Kardashians' show, Kristin was off to France, Lo was working on her new projects and Audrina was getting a reality show all of her own.

The production team had made a huge video of all the trips we had made – to Vegas, Hawaii and all over – with us all in over the years. It was amazing seeing how much we had all grown up in front of the camera. Lauren looked like a little schoolgirl in those early episodes! I was sad that Spencer and Heidi weren't part of those final celebrations, but I understood why they were staying away.

I loved my time on *The Hills*, but now, I was ready for the next step.

10

I was lucky enough to have a few projects already lined up when *The Hills* ended. I now knew enough about celebrity to know that if I wanted to work, I had to get out there and make it happen. I couldn't just lie back and expect people to come to me, while my level of public recognition slowly faded.

It sounds bizarre as reality TV is just being yourself, but one of the elements I had liked most of all about *The Hills* was having a proper job. I enjoyed seeing the schedules, knowing I was needed, that I was part of a team making something successful. I wanted more of that, and I wanted people to know that.

So it was thrilling when only weeks after the end of *The Hills* the team at a production company called Bunim/

Murray said that they wanted to talk about some show ideas with me. Bunim/Murray are huge in the reality TV world now – they are behind *Keeping Up with the Kardashians* and all of the spin-offs from that show, as well as other shows like *Project Runway* and *The Real World*.

We came up with a dating show idea that was basically my dream job: a cross between *The Simple Life* and *The Bachelor*. I was single at the time, after the Josh disaster, and it would have been me and my close friend Ashley Leggat as the stars. Ashley was a Disney kid, who had been in movies and shows with the likes of Hilary Duff and Lindsay Lohan. She's still a very close friend and one I see whenever I can when I head back to LA.

The premise was that we'd cross the country looking for a guy for me as I was sick of the guys in LA and I wanted a nice wholesome country boy. We were going to have a huge caravan and travel from state to state, doing whatever the pastime of that state was for the date. For example, it would have been ice fishing in Alaska. If I liked the guy, he would win a place in the second caravan, which would be travelling behind ours. Then, it was on to the next state. The idea was that after a few weeks I would have a caravan full of hot guys vying for my attention while I travelled around milking cattle and lobster fishing or whatever on further dates.

Yeah, sounds like a tough job, doesn't it?

We made what the industry calls a 'sizzle reel' – a sort of

taster tape – of about five minutes, and it went to the ten major networks. To our delight, it was sold to the Oxygen network. Only four months after the end of *The Hills* and I had a new show to work on – it was the dream! Then came the Christmas break . . .

I don't know what happened, but somebody somewhere decided during Christmas that they didn't want to make the show after all. It was cancelled before it had begun. I was so sad. But I also knew that sitting around feeling blue wasn't going to get me anywhere, so I got myself set up with all the LA agents I needed, and decided to head to the East Coast for a few months.

I loved the response that I always got from New Yorkers. In Los Angeles a lot of people were kind of bored of *The Hills*. It had been showing them their own town, so many of them resented the fact that we had gotten this level of fame by doing very little, and they could treat us as if we were just a bit dreary and exhausting. It was completely different in New York. Whenever I mentioned on Twitter, which I had by now got a little more used to, that I was heading east, my agent would immediately get a flood of restaurants offering to host meals for me, or stores offering credit or discounts if I wanted to go shopping there. In the end I lived in New York for well over a year, popping back every now and then for castings and appearances and to see family. I lived in hotels mostly: the Soho Grand, the Dream Downtown or The MAve Hotel. I had a lot of friends over there, and I also started seeing someone pretty quickly.

I was offered VIP tickets to go and see a Rangers ice hockey game, and while I was there some of the press girls asked me if there was anyone on the team I had my eye on. As a matter of fact, I did. One of them, Michael, was absolutely gorgeous, and, as it turned out, single.

'My God we loooove him,' the girls told me. It was the seal of approval. If he was nice to the press girls that was good enough for me. After the game, I met him in the green room and he asked if I would like to go for a drink with him and some of his team-mates. I was delighted to, and a few days later he came himself to collect me from the hotel I was living in.

It wasn't long before we started dating properly. I went to all of his games, we got really close and I was loving my new New York life. Lo Bosworth was also living there at the time and she would come with me to some of the games – we even set her up with one of Michael's team-mates. It was such a laugh, going out with an old friend and a bunch of the New York Rangers.

The city suited me. I had enough bits of work that I was independent and busy, but not so much that I was buckling under the pressure of fame as I had been during the tougher times on *The Hills*. I would get up, head to pilates, get something healthy to eat from Whole Foods, get myself ready and nearly every day would have lunch with my best

Spencer and Heidi on their wedding day.

Hawaii trip
with Audrina,
Lauren and Lo.

Audrina and
me in Miami.

Hanging out with
Audrina and Lo.

Another Miami trip with
Audrina, Kristin and Lo.

Me on the red carpet
at the MTV movie awards.

Tanning in
Miami with Lo.

My best friend Lucy and me last summer in NYC.

Night out in London with Lucy.

Celebrating my 28th birthday in Notting Hill with my agent Emily, Lucy and Stevie.

My first night in
London... the night I met
Spencer Matthews at
the Grand Prix ball.

With my ex boyfriend
Stevie last summer
in NYC.

Kauai with my favorite people (my parents) 2013.

The night I entered the Celebrity Big Brother house.

And the night I left...

At the London premiere of Tommorrowland with *Josh*.

A favourite selfie in a London black cab.

friend Simon Huck, who I had met at Lo and Lauren's Christmas party and had got to know through the fashion world in LA.

Simon had just become a partner at Command PR, which he now owns and runs. He was working with Jonathan Cheban. Reality fans will know Simon and Jonathan from *Keeping Up with the Kardashians*, and their own show *The Spin Crowd* (which was produced by Kim). We called our meetings 'debriefs' and we'd chat about whatever was the hot gossip of the day, who was in town, or whatever was on our plates.

When your boyfriend is in Manhattan's ice hockey team and your best friend takes care of a lot of the city's lifestyle PR, you have a fun time. And I did. I was eating right, exercising right and having fun. Life was sweet. But not entirely sweet. I wanted to get back to work, too. So I was heading back and forth to LA a lot, for castings and meetings.

Auditions really are not my favourite way to spend time. Well, that's putting it mildly. They are the worst way for me to spend my time. It really is a horrible process. I was going to different types of audition that year: ones for hosting or presenting jobs, and ones for commercials.

Presenting jobs are much more fun, but the auditions are kind of odd. So often presenting is about dealing with an audience, interacting with another presenter, that type of thing. Auditioning to be yourself is a pretty weird process, but having to do it with imaginary people makes it even worse.

You're given a brief on what sort of show it is. A cookery show, an entertainment show, a games show or whatever. And you're told the vibe of the show. 'Okay, there's a lot of money on the line at this point, Stephanie.' And then there's a prompter with your script. But there's no audience. You have to read your lines as if to people, except it's just to empty space; while you're being watched by three or four people who are watching you silently, scribbling ominous-looking notes, and whispering to each other as if they're in the cast of *Flashdance*.

I hated it. I just didn't 'get' it. And I would find it so terrifying that I would always have to wear wedge heels instead of regular high heels as I hated my nervous lower legs giving me away with the shaking.

But presenting auditions were nothing compared to the sheer torture of commercial auditions. Why would I want to do commercials? Well, because you earn a ridiculous amount of money for a relatively small amount of work – they're less than two minutes long! Well, I thought it would be a relatively small amount of work. But I had not factored in the hours of auditions and the torment of going to them. The worst thing was, I was clearly no good at it.

You had to get to the audition for a certain call time. There was no way you could turn up late. If you missed the call time, that was it for you, game over. But you always had to wait. Always. You always knew there would be at least an hour that you'd be sitting around in torment, but that you could never skip that time as turning up for the wrong call time would write you out of the game.

The other girls there would always be jobbing actresses who were trying to make it in Hollywood and were really doing the circuit. A lot of them seemed to be friends and there was a real sense of camaraderie between them. They'd be checking each others' make-up, hugging each other as they went in the room and wishing each other luck and so on.

There was none of that love for me, though. I found it incredibly uncomfortable being in those rooms, knowing that they knew who I was, and that they resented me. I guess I can see why. I was, to them, already famous. Some of them even took out their phones and tried to slyly take photographs of me. They wanted what I had and I'm sure a few of them didn't think I deserved it. I don't blame them really, especially if they were recalling the drama and conflict that so many people associated with *The Hills*. They just wanted a slice of the action and as far as they could see I was swooping in, bringing a level of fame and audience with me, and going in on top of them.

They had no idea how I was performing on the other side of the door, though. My name would be called. There would be a deafening silence as literally no one wished me luck, and I would walk into the room full of directors, assistants and casting agents. They'd all be sitting on a couch, with their snacks and their coffees and their note-pads scattered around. Absolutely no one would greet me, or even acknowledge me. Maybe I am being harsh. I'm sure that perhaps one or two blinked, or even sort of nodded at me.

Someone to the side of the room would say, 'Okay, on three. One two three . . .' and you would have to launch into whatever the script said. Totally cold. Especially bad if you were either doing something ridiculously dramatic, or with someone else who you had only just met.

One especially bad audition was for the Syfy channel. The best I can say about it is that I pray there are no tapes of that audition lying around anywhere. I should have known it wasn't going to be glamorous – the premise was that there was a mutant bug attacking my eye. I had to pretend I was in my bathroom, putting on my make-up, when it attacked me. I could see blood coming out of my eye and I had to start screaming and grabbing at it.

'Argh ARGH MY EYE!!' I was yelling, while trying to express mutant-bug-ness as well as I could by clawing at my face. The casting couch remained silent. One man clicked the lid of his pen on.

'Thank you for your time, Stephanie, we'll be in touch.'

There was another occasion when I had to passionately kiss a stranger. We had met less than a minute before, and I had to turn to him and start kissing him intensely in front of the usual wall of silence. It was so embarrassing. He seemed like a nice guy but doing these things out of context, with no sense of motivation for the characters we were playing, was confusing and demoralising.

I never really got hardened to the process, the way that some proper professional actresses seem to. I would walk out of the room thinking the same thing every time: 'My God that felt horrible but I think I NAILED it.' Every time! I don't know why but I was always convinced that no matter how bad it was, I had always done a really good job. I would often get a callback, but then I'd always fall at the final hurdle.

I guess I had a different take on 'nailed it' than most casting directors did. The job I was most upset not to get was a presenting job: *Fashion Police*. It was down to the final two for that role, me and Kelly Osbourne. And, as you know, it went to Kelly. She only just resigned this year. I wanted to be furious about that, especially after what had happened between us over Josh. But I decided not to think about Kelly much after that . . .

While I was doing all of these auditions, my boyfriend Michael was sent down to the Connecticut Whales from the New York Rangers for a while, to regain his confidence. I felt terrible for him as it must have been quite humiliating for that to happen. So I took the train to Hartford and made sure I was there to support him at his first game. I'd also sent him a nice care package before I arrived to show him how much I cared. I wasn't going to dump him just because he was demoted! Instead I think I was too nice . . . almost like a mom. I was trying to take care of him as his world was falling apart. And he was happy to let me bend over backwards for him, without ever showing any appreciation. Surely that would change though? 'He's going through a hard time,' I told myself, 'he will be nicer.' Blah blah blah.

Valentine's Day had arrived! Things were much better for Michael, he was back playing for the Rangers and I was so excited to be spending our first Valentine's Day in New York City together. I talked to him in the morning and asked what the plan was. I was hoping for a romantic dinner, maybe at Lavo where we'd had our first date. You can imagine my shock when he told me the plan . . . to play video games with his friends. Back then I was trying to be a cool girlfriend. 'Okay, cool,' I would say while secretly raging inside. It's good to be a cool girlfriend but remember, you get what you put up with! Never settle for something you don't deserve. It took me to age twenty-seven to realise that.

Then on my birthday two months later he sent me some powdered Gatorade and some hockey movies. 'He's finally using his imagination,' I thought. 'I can't wait to see what his real present is at the weekend. It's going to be something spectacular after this wind-up!'

I told my mom about his cute plan.

'Honey, I don't think it's a joke,' she said gently.

'Don't be ridiculous, that won't be my real present!' I replied.

'Darling, he's a guy from Canada who lives and breathes hockey. He's not interested in impressing a girl from the TV.'

I didn't care that he didn't want to impress someone from TV, I liked that he liked me for me – but I did want to feel as if he had thought about a present a bit. Tried to connect with me maybe . . . I called my friends, who all reassured me that of course it was a joke, and I was right to be looking forward to a big deal at the weekend.

They were mistaken. We all were, apart from my mom. He really had given me a birthday present better suited to a twelve-year-old boy.

When I confronted him about it, he told me I was going to love powdered Gatorade and he didn't see what the big deal was. I'm afraid we had a bit of a fight. So he sent me a teddy. We'd gone from a present better suited to a twelve-year-old boy to one for an eight-year-old girl. I got the feeling that maybe Michael and I were not going to go the distance.

He was one of the sweetest guys I had ever dated, but he didn't seem to know what a girlfriend was. And I didn't want to teach him, only for him to up and find the love of his life once he realised what a loving relationship could be. I had had a lot of therapy, and a lot of time for self-reflection by then. I was at peace with who I was, I knew what my journey was and I think he was only just starting out getting to know himself – he had been so consumed by sport for so long.

I hadn't helped things by mothering him. I would send him care packages, make sure he was okay after his move away from New York, try to look after him however I could. No wonder he treated me more like a mom than a girlfriend. But it was not enough, and by late spring of 2012 we had split up.

My next boyfriend was a very different kind of guy. That summer Simon and I went on holiday to Europe. Simon was invited to Sardinia, as the guests of an Arab prince – on his yacht. Julien, who was a French Syrian internet entrepreneur, was staying on the yacht as well, with his brother. We started a little love affair that summer and by the time we were back in New York we fell in love really fast.

He was an interesting guy. He was a little bit older than me and had had huge business success by creating the app Line Snob, which let you find out – or tell other people – how big the line was at somewhere you'd need to queue. An iPhone launch or a new club launch or whatever. He was more worldly about things like business and culture so we had a great time together and I learned a lot. He was very charismatic, he became friends with Simon too, and of course as the creator of an app that was about getting to the front of queues, he took me to a lot of fantastic places.

Before too long, he asked me to move in to his apartment in New York. I was so excited. I started to move my stuff and I had my mom sending me things from LA. We were about to begin the process of looking for a new apartment for the two of us. Life could not have been better.

Then one sunny Saturday, after lunch in Soho, we got into an altercation with a cop. We were parked outside of the Mercer Hotel, which often has celebrities staying in it, and as a result often has paparazzi – professional and amateur – waiting outside of it. So the whole incident was videoed by someone who put it on YouTube. The hotel valet had put the car, a ridiculously flashy Ferrari, in a no-parking zone on the road outside of the hotel. As we came to get into it, a cop was writing out a parking-violation ticket. But instead of accepting it, apologising or verbally trying to state his case, Julien got into the car and tried to drive away – while I was still on the sidewalk.

Maybe he could have got away with this if no one had been taping it. More importantly, maybe he could have got away with this if the policeman wasn't standing right next to the car. The policeman shouted that his foot had been driven over. Instead of trying to rectify the situation as calmly as possible, Julien revealed an incredibly aggressive and really quite scary side to him. I had never seen that before, and I did not like it. His blood was absolutely boiling. I knew I had to keep my cool. I did my best in the situation, but I really was not sure if this was the sort of person I wanted to be living with. This was an argument over a $50 parking ticket and he was an app millionaire. If he was going to respond like this to something so trivial, what else was there of his temper that I had yet to see?

Julien was arrested then and there, and Simon and I got him bailed, but he was not allowed out of jail until the Monday. We went home together that day, but despite the charges later being dropped, after that incident nothing was ever the same again. Nor should it have been. I had seen what he could do when challenged.

By now I had a small role doing some presenting back home for Stars Entertainment doing a strand of online TV and showbiz interviews, so the talk of plans for a joint apartment slowly faded and I started to spend more time in LA again. By Christmas we had officially broken up. I dated a couple of guys in LA, but after a run of bad luck I swore off guys for a bit. Ha! Little did I know what lay round the corner for me . . .

During this phase of less-than-ideal relationships, I had also been trying to set up the handbag design company that had been my dream since my early days of studying at FIDM. I had found partners in South Africa who would manufacture the bags, and I had spent a fortune on trademarking the name I wanted: Monroe Bags. I bought unbelievably expensive software to design with, and paid for a number of sample bags to be made in South Africa. Then, after a few months of waiting, never hearing from the manufacturers, and wondering what was going on, they eventually told me that there had been a break-in at the warehouse and the samples had all been stolen. After that my relationship with them broke down and I decided to cut my losses and put the entire enterprise on the back burner for a while.

I learned more than I realised during those couple of years after *The Hills*, acquiring business knowledge and experience, and the certainty that auditions were my worst nightmare. It was time for a change of scene though, and once again it was one of my male buddies who came up with the goods.

11

I had always wanted to visit the UK, so when my friend Michael invited me to be his travel buddy for a tour of Scotland, Ireland and London I said I'd go with him faster than I could say, 'Will it all look like Notting Hill?' As far as I was concerned, London was beautiful, and posh . . . but a lot of fun. I knew Dublin was kind of arty and in Scotland I was obsessed by the Loch Ness Monster, but it was that classy *joie de vivre* I was sure London had that I was really interested in.

Michael had long been my absolute favourite GBF. I'd met him via TV, as he used to work on *Saturday Night Live*, and now he lived in Hawaii. Kind, interesting and always hilarious, I knew he was the perfect person to take a trip with. And the UK was somewhere I had wanted to go for so long. I knew this trip would be good. But I had no idea how good . . . or why.

Before we set off, I was mostly preoccupied with my packing. I had a kind of English Rose look I was after. Some headscarves, a nice bit of blusher, nothing too LA. But my brother Spencer was more interested in who I was going to hang out with in London. He had decided to give my details to some other Spencer. Spencer Matthews.

Apparently he knew Spencer from when he and Heidi had been in the UK earlier in 2013 doing *Celebrity Big Brother*. Spencer Matthews had made contact with him on Twitter, and he seemed like a bit of a super-fan. He had kept on at him, 'I'm your biggest fan', 'We have to meet', 'You're my idol, a true epic villain, I've loved you since *The Hills*.' You get the idea. He had kept on at my brother with the 'I'm dying to meet you . . .' until eventually Spencer and Heidi caved (and possibly did a bit of Googling), and said yes.

They were staying at The Dorchester on Park Lane and invited him to dinner at China Tang. When they met him they realised he was 'kind of a big deal' in reality TV in the UK. It would have been nice if Heidi and Spencer had actually made this clear to me, too, though . . .

Instead, I got an email from my brother saying that I 'had to meet this guy Spencer Matthews' and sorting out our contact details. 'My sister's coming to London for the first time, can you let her know what the hotspots are so she has a good time,' he had said. And Spencer replied saying he'd love to and he'd be in touch nearer the time. My brother gave me a bit of an airy wave, and said something about how he'd know all the good clubs, but did he elaborate? No he did not.

And let's get one thing straight: Spencer Pratt's radar for who the 'great guys' are is not to be trusted. The last time he put me in touch with one of his 'great guy' super-fans, it was not a huge success. He was a guy who worked in technology, wore a Homer Simpson T-shirt and told me he hated tipping. Charming he was not. People get weirdly obsessed with Spencer and Heidi, behaving very differently around them than they do around the rest of us, so their hot tips on people I 'must meet' go largely ignored by me. All in all, I had developed a pretty good filter system for my brother's 'badge of quality'. In all honesty, I doubted I would ever meet this Spencer Matthews 'fellow'.

But then . . . the day we left the States I got an email from Mr Matthews asking when we were going to land and where we were staying. I replied, in brief, trying to keep a distance from the super-fan.

'Well, the evening you get in there is a ball I would love to take you to – would you like to accompany me?'

Um, helloooo?

Would I, Miss Stephanie Pratt, like to go to a ball? On my first night in England? I think so.

So I pulled out all the stops. I know a ball is just what

we'd call a dinner in the US, but still – it was London so it was a ball! I made a huge effort – an A.L.C. dress, Alexander McQueen pink shoes, a spray tan and a proper blow-dry. Michael was coming, too, and was most entertained by my excitement, which didn't dip at all when Spencer sent a Mercedes to the W Hotel in London's Leicester Square to collect us.

'Wow!' I said to Michael. 'The English charm isn't just a myth!'

When we arrived there were security checks and lists after lists before our car was allowed through the gates. It felt like I had stepped into James Bond's world, and with every passing minute I was more and more glad that I had made the effort with my clothes. Still, when we got out of the car I was on the lookout for a nerd in nylon who was maybe wearing a *Family Guy* T-shirt.

I have never been more happy to be wrong. As we pulled up at what looked like an amazing country home, we saw someone standing on the red carpet, waving at us.

'Oh. My. God,' I said to Michael.

'Is that him?!' he replied.

'He is SO hot!'

And hot he was. Wearing a deep-blue Dior suit with a black bow tie, and a grin that could charm the birds from the trees, he was smiling at me as he opened the door to the Mercedes. He seemed to know what I looked like, and I was starting to wish I had Googled him. Even as we got out of the car, both Michael and I were still muttering, 'So hot, so very hot, so very very hot . . .'

We might have been surprised by how easy Spencer was on the eye but one thing was for sure – he knew it. And that was one of the most attractive things about him. He knew he looked good and he knew he had invited me to a great event. And on top of that, as he kissed me hello and led me to the red carpet . . . he knew we looked good together. His confidence is part of his charm, and it was a good thing as he oozes it from every pore. I was weak at the knees by the time we reached the red carpet. Just totally overwhelmed by his looks, his accent, his charming smile.

All of a sudden a bank of photographers was calling his name and pointing at me.

'Guys! Guys! Will you take a picture together!', 'Show us your date, Spencer!', 'Stephanie, over here!'

At first it was all a bit much but in seconds (and with only half a smile from Spencer) I thought, 'Why not? I'm at a BALL! With a really hot guy!' To this day the pictures from that event are some of my favourite ever, but . . .

I had no idea then why everyone was so excited to see him with a new girl that night. I was blissfully unaware that Spencer was one of the absolute stars of the hit show *Made in Chelsea*, and that he had pretty much forged a career out of being seen with the prettiest girls in town on his arm, before cheating on them or replacing them faster than his underwear. Much less did I know that he had just broken up with a girl called Lucy Watson, on TV. No idea.

I have never, ever known anything like the paparazzi scrum that we had that night. If we had turned up in the most elaborate Halloween costumes ever I still don't think we would have got as much attention. Now, I like a compliment as much as the next girl, but to me, this was baffling. Even as we walked into the ball, Michael a few steps behind, chuckling to himself, every single table stared and whispered as we passed. To this day I have never been to an event like that one. It was like something from a movie – even if it was a movie I had missed the first half of.

We had the best time that night, with fun and glamour in equal measure. The ball was the Grand Prix ball, to celebrate the racing event coming to London. It was held at the Hurlingham Club, the sort of place I had only imagined existed. It's a private members' club just south of Chelsea, on the banks of the Thames. It has that creamy wedding cake façade that looks like something from a Jane Austen novel, and is set in acres of beautifully manicured lawns. From the moment we were greeted with champagne to the moment we all headed out for drinks at Morton's in Mayfair, central London, afterwards, it felt like I had stepped into a classic English story book. There was a gourmet dinner, The Feeling played live, and we were surrounded by motor sport legends. Not that I had eyes for anyone else as my attention had truly been grabbed. In true fairy tale style, of course I ended up back at Spencer's. No, I didn't sleep with him but there was no way I was going to be able to see him go home alone that night, even if it meant Michael did.

The next morning the charm was still beaming out of him. He rolled over and said, 'What do you want to do today?' and I knew instantly. 'I want to get Mexican food and I want to see a movie.'

So we headed back to the W Hotel, me still in my outfit from the night before. This outfit had by now been online in some of the newspapers, so as I walked in with Spencer on my arm I can only imagine what the doormen at the hotel thought. My best guess would be, 'Oh no, this girl is his next poor victim.' Still, I was oblivious, and fast entering the love bubble.

I got into the shower while Spencer caught up with Michael. By the time I was out of the shower he had raided the minibar and was necking tiny vodkas. The guy was an animal. It was only 11.00 am! Once I was ready we all walked across Leicester Square and watched *World War Z*, before heading to Chiquito for food and margaritas. (Spencer passed out for the whole of the movie, which in hindsight should perhaps have been an early red flag.)

We just could not keep our hands off each other. We

were that couple in the restaurant, putting everyone else off their food. Michael was amazingly tolerant, and even went as far as to take some cute pictures on his phone.

Finally, over this meal, some of the details about Spencer's profile in the UK started to click. The photos from the night before had gone everywhere, and people on Twitter were asking about some Lucy girl, so he explained that he had cheated on this girl and broken up with her – but she had been a hideous, possessive nightmare. Poor Spencer, I thought, as I stroked his face again. She sounds like a witch.

From that day onwards we were inseparable for the rest of the summer. We spent every day and every night together, apart from my already planned trips to Scotland and Ireland with Michael. Those trips were a hoot in themselves with Michael and I heading up to Glasgow on the train for his girl friend's wedding. I was his date and we had an incredible time at the Blythswood Square hotel, and getting fully Scottish for the wedding! We were total tourists, visiting the Trump Turnberry hotel and spa, doing the whole of Edinburgh and then getting into the gay bars of Dublin as the next leg of the trip. Once I was back in London, people took photos of Spencer and me wherever we went, with our relationship spreading like Twitter wildfire, as we were followed by paparazzi more and more. They were crazy days.

While Spencer was filming *Made in Chelsea*, Michael

and I headed out and did all of the touristy things we had come to London to do – Big Ben, the London Eye, Harrods – and then every night we would all go out together. Michael was pretty good about putting up with my constant texting all day, but he and Spencer got on so well, he had a great time in the evenings, too. The more time I spent with Spencer, the more I realised why he had been such a fan of my brother: they have exactly the same sense of humour – our family's sense of humour. I thought we were perfect for each other. As far as I was concerned he was 'the one'. And I have never felt that way so fast, and so certainly with anyone in my life.

I had more fun that summer than I had had in years. And all when it had been so completely unexpected: I found love on my first night. I came to London for a holiday but the reality had been so much more fun. I was in love with the perfect English gentleman, who also shared my sense of humour. What more could I have asked of London?

Little did I know what was just around the corner . . .

By now I was familiar with *Made in Chelsea*, having heard enough about it from Spencer and – finally – having done a bit of Googling of my own. What I wasn't expecting was for Spencer to tell me one sunny afternoon that the producers of the show really wanted to meet me. They were about to start filming the antics of the group of friends for the sixth series, and apparently they were keen to have me on board, too. I wasn't so sure. After all, I had already been on a reality show before.

To add insult to injury, this Lucy girl he'd been telling me about kept popping up everywhere calling me a fake. Seriously, why could she not just shut up? In every weekly magazine and every online gossip site I had seen in the UK, there she was, sulking and going on about how our relationship was a sham, it was all vanity, there was nothing in it and whatever else she thought might stick. Why was she clinging to Spencer's coat-tails like this? And how was I supposed to be in a sham relationship when I didn't even know who he was when I got together with him? As well as her, there was some Louise woman – another ex – who kept chipping in, too. Most of all, I didn't want to meet Lucy, let alone share a screen with her.

Whether or not I decided to let the *MiC* cameras in on my life, I couldn't get out of meeting some more of Spencer's friends. Inevitably, this included Louise Thompson, who Spencer was on slightly better terms with, although he still had some pretty choice words about her. We went to a charity event held by Francis Boulle's mother, with Michael, who was still in town. I was wearing a gorgeous silver sequinned dress from All Saints that I had bought in Harvey Nichols especially for the event. I felt good – the dress was like sparkly armour to protect me from whatever exes might be thrown at me that night. I wanted to be kind, though. I considered myself to be the lucky one at that point, with Spencer as mine-all-mine, so I didn't want to be making any heartbroken girls feel bad about themselves. Smugness is not charming, I told myself, and resolved to be kind all evening.

When I was introduced to Louise the first thing I was surprised by was how tiny she is! Seriously, she is barely five feet tall, and she is just the cutest thing. She seemed quite sensitive, maybe still quite vulnerable, so I really made an effort to be polite and charming. When I went to the bathroom, I even extended the ultimate girly hand of friendship – I asked her to come along, too, so we could chat.

And we did chat. We had a great time talking about New York City and how much we both loved it there, while carefully avoiding the topic we really had in common. I thought she was really sweet, and not at all the evil witch that Spencer had told me she was. How exhausting it must have been for him to keep trying to keep us all apart, telling us untruths about each other . . . I didn't know that was his game back then, though, so I kept my distance a little bit. I was looking for peace, not a new friendship.

In the end I decided that taking part in the show for a bit couldn't be that bad after all. They wanted me so much, they told us we were such a great couple, and I was so infatuated with him that I felt my anxieties falling away the longer we all talked. I was a very different person from when I appeared on *The Hills*. I had had a career, I had been off drugs for years now, rather than just months. And I had a far greater sense of who I was and what I could cope with. I was going to be part of the *Made in Chelsea* team: a new chapter in my life. But would it mean new friends or new enemies?

The first person that I met once I had landed back in the UK after a brief trip abroad to sort out some visa issues was Lucy's friend Binky Felstead. We bumped into her walking her dog while Spencer and I were on our way back from the airport. I could feel suspicion dripping off her, and she was practically calling her friends with all the gossip on me while we were still talking. I tried not to let it fluster me, though – after all, I was with Spencer and I was no threat to her. The real threat was Lucy, who I was due to meet a few days later.

The occasion when I knew I would be meeting pretty much everyone was the Guards polo in Windsor. I was delighted to be taking part in an event that seemed so entirely British – especially one with horses! And Pimm's! It was an event I spent days preparing for, as I wanted to get just the right look. I wore a printed floral dress from Sandro. I wanted to bring to mind a bit of a Julia Roberts in *Pretty Woman* vibe with the cut and the flowing fabric of the skirt. I knew it had to be something that covered my knees and I knew I wanted colour. I was also mindful not to wear spiked heels so I didn't spend the day sliding back into the grass. I got some gorgeous chunky-heeled Paul Smith shoes and smiled serenely while other girls there had to spend their time on tiptoes, clinging to the men's shoulders to stop themselves sinking backwards.

Outfit aside, it was horribly tense once we got there. By that point I had only met Spencer, Francis and Louise and her then boyfriend Andy Jordan. The rest were strangers, and getting to know any of them was not helped by Lucy shooting me the dirtiest looks I have ever seen. This wasn't just plain old side eye – her trying to get the measure of me while hoping I wouldn't notice. These were full-on filthy looks aimed directly at me. I kept myself calm, and despite the heat and my new-found love of Pimm's, I managed to ignore the glances being fired my way.

I suppose I should have realised at the time, but it took me a while to understand that the day was much harder for her than it was for me. From my point of view, she was the one who had it easy as she was on home turf, and was surrounded by her friends. But all she could see was that I was here to stay. The new girlfriend, who had been all over the press all summer, was now infiltrating her social group, her show, her life. She had slagged me off in public thinking she would never have to meet me. And now, here I was, smiling sweetly with a Pimm's in my hand and 'her' guy on my arm.

In the end though I'd had enough of her faces and decided to go and confront her. I walked over and said, 'Hey, I've met everyone else here, and I know you're Lucy. I haven't met you yet.' She mumbled something or other and continued looking sulky. I asked her why she had been giving me such dirty looks and she told me that that was just what her face looked like.

Within moments she told me that Spencer had cheated on her eight times when they had been dating. She told me that, like me, she had lived in his apartment and he had cheated on her while she had been there. She said that it wasn't just a case of him having a wandering eye when he went abroad or to different cities for events, but that he would go out for a few hours, have sex with someone else and then come home while she was still there watching TV. It was such a horrible, disgusting story, I wouldn't believe that the lovely Spencer I knew would do this to anyone, let alone to her – as she increasingly seemed like a decent person.

I had never been cheated on by anyone at this point. So when Lucy told me these home truths, my eyes welled up with tears. It is one thing to read something in a magazine or online and think, 'Well, this bitch has never even met me, she doesn't have a clue what my relationship is like.' It's quite another to have them standing there, looking you in the eye, looking heartbroken and intensely vulnerable. I could see how much pain was there: she was a fragile person who had been hurt, not just an evil, jealous, scare-mongering cow.

My mouth was hanging open and my eyes were still full of tears when Spencer strutted up to defend me. Right off the bat he was telling Lucy to leave me alone, and trying to terminate our conversation, but what I really felt like was hugging Lucy. I could not believe how nasty his tone was, and how much cruelty had been revealed to be lying there, just beneath the surface. How on earth did he dare to speak to her with that tone when he had treated her so savagely? Why was he not more ashamed around her?

As we drove home from the polo that evening I could not stop thinking about the confrontation, and slowly the penny dropped. He had not been protecting me from her meanness all of those months. He had been protecting me from the truth. About him. I longed to call her and continue our conversation, but I realised I didn't have Lucy's number. And I certainly wasn't going to get it from Spencer. As the car turned into his street that evening I realised I was rather alone, and it freaked me out. Michael had returned to the States and Spencer had begged me to stay with him at his house, even when I offered to move into a nearby hotel. I had committed to *Made in Chelsea* for at least a few weeks. So I was alone in London living with a man I had just seen a very upsetting side to. Everything had changed . . .

12

Spencer may have said that he wanted me around, but it suddenly started to feel like that wasn't really the case. He now seemed like a lonely person who always needed to have someone on hand, but who also wanted to be able to come and go as he pleased.

'I'll keep an eye on you,' was what he had told me when I offered to stay at the nearby Blakes hotel after Michael headed back to the States. He made it sound as if he wanted to look after me. I can look after myself, but I wanted him to be happy. Now, it was clear that he wanted to keep an eye on me, but he was far from keen on me keeping an eye on him.

Two nights after the hideous day at the polo event he went out and never came home. I woke up in his bed the next morning, alone and confused. His phone was turned off, there was no way to reach him. At last, I received a text message that he had 'gone out and fallen asleep at Fred's house'. I had no idea who Fred was. I've never heard of him since. I didn't really care. But even a massive party animal can get themselves home to bed – from anywhere in London or beyond. It's not as if he was a student who had missed the last tube and couldn't afford a cab. If he'd wanted to be at home, he would have been. There was no reason for him to have stayed out.

To make matters worse, we were both due at a huge party that night. It was a spectacular Bollywood party for Victoria Baker-Harber's birthday, which was being held at Jewel Piccadilly. I had been looking forward to it for a couple of weeks, and was keen to see Lucy and talk to her a bit more, too. I had been with Phoebe-Lettice Thompson and Louise to get our special Bollywood-themed dresses and we all had plans to get our hair and make-up done first as well. I called the girls, who I was now starting to form friendships of my own with, and said that I wasn't going to make it. After all, I still had no idea when Spencer was actually planning to come home. Would I even see him before the party?

It turned out that the answer to that was a resounding no. I was persuaded to go to the party despite my reservations, but did not see Spencer until he showed up there. And when I did see him, his response made my blood run cold. He tried to brush me off, to make out that I was being princess-y or needy.

'Since when were you the fun police?' he asked with a petulant little sneer. I told him that his behaviour was not okay. I did sincerely believe that this was a one-off. I was having my boundaries tested. I was keen not to overreact, but to be firm. He should not feel that he could get away with whatever he wanted, but nor should he feel that I didn't want him ever to leave the house. There is a middle ground . . . for most normal people . . . I hated being at that party, but it was great to see the girls again, and as we headed home (with Spencer nodding off beside me) I felt confident that I had knocked his crap behaviour on the head. I had put my foot down. Lucy had clearly never managed to do this.

The next morning he pulled the apologies out of the bag in spectacular style: he whisked me off on an incredible trip to the South of France. We stayed with his godfather in a beautiful villa in Nice. I met some more of his extended family – so many of whom I had already got to know. He was, after all, the guy who had taken me home to meet all of his brothers, sisters, nieces and nephews within a week of us being together. While we were in France I felt safe in his company again, and confident that the episode the previous week had been a nasty one-off that I had now made clear could not happen again. Something wasn't quite right though – I spent more time hanging out with his godmother than him while we were in Nice and by the time we got back to London there was a friendly – but noticeable – distance between us.

A few days after our return, I was meeting him for drinks at a little bar in Chelsea. He had been out all day, while I had stopped into Joe & the Juice for a sandwich, been to Zara and bought myself a cute new outfit that I was now wearing, and been in touch with my mom about whether I might come home for Thanksgiving and Christmas. It was looking like I probably would.

Confusingly, when I walked into the bar, I saw Lucy and Louise sitting there. Weird. Why were they here and not Spencer? I hadn't seen Lucy since the Bollywood party and even that had been very brief. I sat down with my heart in my mouth and a terrible feeling that I knew what was coming.

My guess was right. As soon as I heard the words, 'But you guys weren't exclusive, right?' I had it confirmed that what I had feared and suspected was right. Spencer had been cheating on me. The girls reassured me that I wasn't alone, and that he had done it to both of them, but it wasn't much consolation. I was more stunned than angry or upset. We were no longer spending time together like we had been in the summer, and it's never a good sign if you start having more fun with your boyfriend's family than with him.

I asked Louise how she knew it was true and she explained that when Spencer and her brother Sam had been to Dublin together for a personal appearance, Spencer had decided to spend two extra unnecessary nights there, staying in the same hotel. Louise explained that she had looked through Sam's phone (the privilege of a nosey older sister) and had seen a text from Sam to Spencer saying, 'Are you ready to meet in the lobby?'

Spencer's reply had said, 'Yeah I'm just trying to get this bird out of my room.'

That was pretty conclusive. It was way too detailed to be made up. I didn't question her for a second.

Just as I heard that, Spencer walked in. He wasn't too happy to see me sitting with his two exes and his facial expression made that more than clear. He wasn't getting his own way and he didn't like it one bit. When he sat down to talk to me, he had the same tone of voice with me that I had heard him use when he'd addressed Lucy at the polo match. Nasty and cold-hearted.

The girls got up to leave, and I was left with Spencer and his babyish 'Well, what did you think would happen?' attitude. The way he saw it, I had suffocated him by moving in with him – even though it had been him that had begged me to go with that arrangement – so he had made it his business to stop spending time at home. He's just the kind of guy who will avoid a situation entirely if it may potentially be uncomfortable. As Lucy had warned me would happen, he was taking zero responsibility for his own actions and making me do all of the emotional dirty work. When

Spencer wants to break up with a girl, he avoids all confrontation; he simply cheats and hopes they get the message. As ever, he didn't have the balls to say he'd like to go back to the bachelor life, he just cheated and hoped I'd find out. This left me being the strait-laced one wanting a level of emotional commitment, me making the difficult decisions, and me having to take the pain of rejection without the dignity of a proper conversation.

I passed him my copy of his keys and flew home to LA the following day. Life is too short to hang around assholes.

When I landed in LA I looked at my UK phone briefly before turning it off and switching to my US number. It was full of messages from Spencer: he was sorry, he had fucked it all up, he missed me, he wanted to marry me. I sighed, exhausted. I was delirious with jet lag and drained by the last few weeks of having my confidence slowly chipped away at. I had never been cheated on before and I did not care for it one little bit. The whole thing had been horribly exhausting and I just did not want to think about it for a while.

But the messages did not stop. He kept on texting and calling. He said that they were all going to South Africa and he wanted me to go with them. I replied in brief; I wanted to see if he really did mean all of these things, or if he was just a little lonely at home by himself. After a few more days, the contact dried up. I had been right. He didn't want to spend forever with me, he just didn't have the emotional equipment to make it through an episode of *Top Gear* without someone around to keep him company. Boohoo.

I stayed in bed for a week after that, doing little more than eating macaroni cheese and crying. It had been a horrible end to what had been a fantastic trip to London, but at the very least I consoled myself that I was just sad, rather than feeling the old call of addiction. Even if I was back home, I had come far emotionally. I had adored London, and the people, but it all seemed very far away now. Those new friendships would never develop and I was so sad to have that era of my life cut short. My sister thought otherwise, though, and pointed out that staying in bed with no more than cheesy pasta for company would only make me more depressed. As ever, she was right, and slowly I started reconnecting with all of my LA friends and going out again. It was awful to have left on a bad note, but it was great to see my family, my friends and my three dogs again. I didn't really tell anyone what had happened between Spencer and me, and very few people knew I had been on a TV show in the UK at all. It was in the past. There was no need to know. I pretended it was all a bad dream and never looked back. It was like the summer had never happened and normal life could resume once again.

To a certain degree, it did. I had a wonderful Thanksgiving with all of my family, we had a great Christmas and I went to Tahoe with a group of friends for New Year's Eve too. I just stopped thinking about London, really. Until one afternoon in January I received a weird text.

'Hey Stephanie, it's Lucy Watson. I am in LA and I wanted to know if you would like to meet up.'

How very curious, I thought to myself. We weren't really close; we had only met a few times. What could she want from me?

I immediately called my mom to see what she thought. She said that we should definitely meet, quite rightly pointing out that without her honesty I might still be living in London being made a fool of by Spencer. It was a solid point. Lucy had been way kinder to me than she had needed to be, no matter how many dirty glances she had cast my way at first.

'Welcome to LA! I would love to meet you,' I replied. And we made plans for lunch the next day. Then, to my shame, when I woke up I lost my nerve entirely and ended up flaking out on her. I didn't really want to be bothered by all that London stuff again; it had made me too sad. I couldn't handle reliving it. Lucy seemed okay about it and we rescheduled for the next day. I bailed again. I still could not deal with a London face on my territory, where I had just got back to feeling safe. I told her something had come up. The third time, I knew I couldn't carry on like this. It was her second-to-last day, and I didn't want to be a bitch. I arranged to meet her at her hotel.

As I drove to pick her up, I called Michael and told him where I was and what I was up to. He was the only person beyond my immediate family who really knew what had gone on in London and I knew he would be up for the gossip of Lucy being in town and us going on a lunch date. As I saw her emerge from the hotel lobby I babbled, 'Okay call you back, call you back,' as fast as I could and checked my hair in my mirror. Lucy looked great. She was wearing a yellow floral jumpsuit with a black hat and black boots. I was in printed jeans, Miu Miu shoes and a little denim jacket. She got in the car and we kissed each other coolly, before heading off for lunch.

I drove us to Nobu in Malibu, where I had made us a booking, while we caught up with what she was doing in LA and how she had been enjoying it. She was on vacation, hanging out with a guy and enjoying herself a whole lot while the UK weather was at its worst. It wasn't until we had sat down in Nobu, facing each other and looking each other in the eye, that we said, almost at the same time, 'I can't believe he fucking did it again.'

I had promised myself that I wouldn't dive straight into talking about the whole situation all over again, but it just felt sooooo good to be talking to someone about it. I got right into it, after bottling it up for months since I had left London. Hearing those feelings articulated out loud, to someone who really understood what it felt like, was fantastic. She had been through the exact same thing, and she could have been all, 'See ya later bitch, you made your bed now you've got to lie in it', but she just was not. She didn't leave me to wallow, she didn't laugh at me for what I had believed, and best of all, she was a really good laugh.

The chats we had that day felt like a big hug. It was so great to be able to confide in her – even if it was pretty grim when we realised that Spencer had basically followed the same template with both of us. He had taken her to the South of France after their first big argument, as if it were some emergency ejector seat out of a bad spell, and he had taken her to all of the same restaurants – and the same tables at those restaurants – while he had been wooing her. The more we chatted the more we realised how little he had thought about either of us, and it felt better to know that at least there was no malice there. Just a childish man.

By the time we were driving back from the restaurant we were giggling like old friends. She felt like a sister already. I did not want her go back, so we made another date for breakfast the next day, too. We met at the Urth Caffé in Santa Monica and I took Lucy to the Third Street Promenade shopping area where she got some souvenirs and bits from the iconic LA store Kitson. One of them was a California pillow that she still has on her couch to this day. When I said goodbye to her that day I felt terribly sad, but so happy to have found a real friend in the situation. We kept in touch for all of January – our WhatsApp accounts were in constant use as we shared gossip and news. Then, a couple of opportunities in the spring made me think that perhaps it was time to head back to London after all.

The first was that it was Lucy's birthday in February and I knew she would be celebrating in style. I also knew that if we were going to stay proper friends I should make the effort to go and see her – especially after flaking on her so many times when she was in my home city. An LA friend of mine, Eric, was interested in making a trip to Italy and had been trying to persuade me to go, so crossing the Atlantic for two great reasons seemed increasingly appealing. Then there was the thought that I still had unfinished business with Spencer. It was niggling at me, the way that I had left town in the autumn. I had made it too easy for him. So when I heard that there was going to be a ball in the spring with the whole *MiC* gang attending, my mind was made up. London hadn't seen the last of me after all.

As I arrived at the airport I felt my heart in my throat – a combination of nostalgia for the happiness I had known in London the first time round, despite how misguided so much of it had been, as well as nerves for the upcoming confrontation with Spencer. It felt great to be reunited with Lucy, though, and we had a blast at her birthday party. Then, the night that I was due to confront Spencer, I was shaking with nerves. My friends kept trying to offer me champagne, but I knew that I had to have an absolutely clear head to say what I needed to and to say it as clearly as possible to get him out of my mind, my heart and my life once and for all.

As I let rip, telling him exactly what I thought of the way he had treated me, I realised how much I had grown since the confrontations I had had with Brody back in *The Hills*. I was so much stronger now, so much more confident, and so much surer about what I wanted to put out there of myself. As I lay my head on my pillow that night, I knew that London brought out the best in me, and decided to look for a short-term place to rent the very next day. I'm not going to let a silly boy run me out of the greatest city in the world.

It did not take long and soon I was in a rented apartment in Notting Hill, ready to spend at least the spring in my beloved London. Before long the blossom was out in the pretty candy-coloured streets of Chelsea and Notting Hill, and it really did feel as if the city was smiling at me. I had known all my life that I adored London, and since I had come back from Paris I had longed to live here but never really known how to make it happen. Finally, I was here, and I was determined to make the most of it.

When I was an unhappy teenager in California, unsure of my identity and what my place in the world was, London always seemed like a fantasyland to me. Everyone I admired – Kate Moss, Gwyneth Paltrow, Gwen Stefani – all seemed to be enjoying life in London, while looking incredible the entire time. It was a blur of Guy Ritchie films, Cool Britannia fashion shoots, Madonna having a British accent and endless Get the London Look Rimmel lipsticks. And ever since my first visit the city has not disappointed.

I love that it is as vibrant and interesting as New York City, but that it always feels cleaner and safer. I love that you can walk everywhere, down historic streets and through pretty squares instead of having the eternal loneliness of heading for your car like you have to in LA. Even the simplest things please me: the parks in the summer, the view across the river, crossing the Albert Bridge at night and seeing the endless fairy lights twinkling on the water, getting a cab home and passing the Houses of Parliament and seeing the Ferris Wheel (that's what I call the London Eye) right there. I love heading to the pub to warm up after a winter walk, and sitting in a pretty pub garden with a Pimm's on a summer's day. I love the weather and the way that it is so much more romantic. In California we're always outside, and great as that is, it's no good if all you want to do is to curl up with someone. England does cosiness so well! There is nothing better than a lie-in then watching a film with someone who has stolen your heart, while the rain pours down outside. It is romance beyond romance. I even love watching soccer and rugby (which I finally understand) now!

And I love British food – from The Wolseley to Wetherspoons. I'm serious! While Michael and I were in

Scotland during my first trip to the UK, when we had gone to Glasgow for that wedding, we were determined to find some classic fish and chips. We saw the loveliest old building, with quaint gold and green writing on it, and headed inside for our glamorous first ever taste of the famous dish. I even took a picture and posted it on Twitter! It was only later that I saw all the replies from people openly laughing at me, saying that we were in a Wetherspoons, and that it was not a traditional olde tavern. Even though I know it's not meant to be the classiest of places, I still love them, as well as Pret A Manger – which I am obsessed with, Costa – which I adore, Wagamama – which should definitely exist in LA, and Joe & the Juice – which does the best things with tuna ever. I had my first cream tea in Harrods that summer and discovered the unreal taste of clotted cream. It sounds as dangerous as it is!

As for nights out, that spring I discovered that there is more to life than just the Bluebird, gorgeous though it is. I found fun in Bodo's Schloss, Boujis on a Monday night and Raffles. It was night after night of dressing up, heading for dinner, hitting a club and ending in the small hours in Vingt-Quatre, spilling the beans on the events of the night. I think I would have fallen in love with London itself if I hadn't had my eye caught by someone else that spring.

Sometime around his birthday, I started to see Stevie Johnson as more than just a friend. When I had been with Spencer I had barely known him, but hanging with that group while living in my own place away from the restrictions I had had before, I had gotten to know him much better. And as I had just been treated so badly and he is just the loveliest man in the world, I slowly felt my emotions towards him turn to more than just friendship. We became an item and rather than just cut things short, I decided to extend my stay in London to more than just a month. We spent a lot of time together and he grew to mean a huge amount to me.

This went on for a couple of months, but in the end the lease on the place I had been renting came up, and I had to head back to the States at least for a bit. I had already been approached about entering the *Celebrity Big Brother* house for their summer season, though – so while I was sworn to secrecy about it as part of my contract, I knew that I would be back and that my relationship with Stevie still had a really strong chance of picking back up later in the summer. I wanted to tell him about *Big Brother*, but I knew I couldn't, so I flew home with a heavy but hopeful heart.

Not long afterwards I heard from Lucy that the *MiC* group, including Stevie, were coming to New York City for the summer and I immediately made plans to surprise them there. They were in my country at last, and in a city where I had lived for years, so of course I had to make the effort to come to town and show them around! I was thrilled and immediately set about making plans and stealthily trying to coordinate when and where they would be for the biggest surprise – me visiting them in New York!

But it was me who got the surprise, as by the time I got there, Stevie was already seeing someone else. I had had no idea, and felt my heart fall to the floor when he told me. I'd asked him so many times if he was single and he always told me that he wasn't dating anyone and that he missed me. I felt so embarrassed that I had showed up.

Once again, my heart felt like it had taken a bit of a battering, but at least this time I had something very concrete and extremely distracting to head towards. And this time I wouldn't have to worry about whether or not anyone was or wasn't texting me with apologies and proposals. I was off to the *Celebrity Big Brother* house.

13

I suppose you could say that I wasn't quite prepared for *Celebrity Big Brother*. And you'd be right. I knew that Spencer and Heidi had been on it the previous year, and that they had had quite good fun. But I didn't know much more than that.

I had been back on *Made in Chelsea* as a regular cast member for a while now, and one of the *CBB* producers had got in touch with my agent after chatting to my brother Spencer about whether I might be interested in becoming a contestant, too. The first thing I did was ring Spencer and Heidi to see what they thought of the idea. They were really encouraging, and said I should take the opportunity. I just had a few questions.

'When does the cleaner come? You never see them on the show.'

'There is no cleaner. You have to do it yourself.' Spencer is not one to mince his words.

'Wait, what? But there are so many of you in there . . .!'

'I know, it's gross. But you don't have much else to do all day . . .' Heidi tried to see the bright side.

'And what about laundry? My apartment in Notting Hill doesn't have a dryer so my towels are all crunchy all the time.'

'No dryer,' said Spencer.

'And no washing machine,' followed Heidi. 'You have to wash your own clothes in the bathtub.'

This sounded crazy – there was no way I was going to do it! After years of my life being really out of control, one thing I really need to keep myself sane is clean things around me. I am pretty much germaphobic. I started to tell Spencer and Heidi that this situation was not going to work for me but they persuaded me that I would be able to manage, so, with them behind me all the way, I decided to go in.

As the show approached, they also gave me loads of advice on what kinds of clothes to take in and Heidi explained that I should take enough underwear and sleeping clothes that I wouldn't have to wash any at all while in there. One thing they didn't advise me on was whether to – or how to – have any sort of strategy for success in the house. As far as I was concerned, I was going to a sort of fun summer camp after the sadness of the Stevie situation. I blocked all thoughts of dirty showers from my mind and focussed on all the talk I had heard from Spencer and Heidi about entertaining games and pranks and getting to know more British people. It would be fun! I told myself. How could it not be? Oh, I should have known that there's always a catch . . .

Once contracts had been confirmed and the week the show started was upon me, I was required to head to a hotel in central London, where I would be staying in secret for a couple of days. While there, the days were crammed full of all sorts of photo shoots and interviews for the show itself. We had to take all of the photographs for our phone number when people were going to vote, and the little films of us pleading not to be booted out. And we had to have all of the interviews to make our entrance videos introducing us to the audience.

Most fun of all were the endless questionnaires and mini-tasks to set everything up for the in-house tasks and activities. There was a team of really fun young people who I spent hours with: singing, dancing, doing silly physical tasks, answering daft questions. I guess they were building a sort of profile of which sorts of tasks would be fun for us, make good TV for the viewers, and be manageable for them. I didn't really care what the specifics were, or what the point of all these activities were, as it was a real laugh, and made me much more relaxed about going into the *Celebrity Big Brother* house.

Next, I was provided with a nickname. A couple of days before it goes live the team working on the show start to refer to the contestants not by their names, but by nicknames. For that season, we were all types of UK candy, and I was Skittles. This was to stop us from overhearing the other contestants' names – we were all moved into the same hotel the weekend before, being kept apart from each other and kept away from the media, who were starting to guess who would be taking part this season. All of the *CBB* team were constantly wearing headphones and walkie-talkies to communicate with each other, so it would only have taken an hour or so for me to have known at least half of my future 'rivals' if we hadn't been given the nicknames.

Once I had my new name, I was delivered two suitcases. Into these, I had to fit everything I would be taking with me for what might be a few days or might be three weeks. We were advised to have eight fancy outfits, for parties and eviction nights, and more casual stuff for the rest of the time. One thing that had made me fret when I was doing my shopping was what to wear at night. I normally just sleep in panties, but I didn't want to seem slutty – and I didn't want to be showing too much on TV. Then again, I did not want to be boiling hot every night if I was sleeping in a room with so many other people. In the end I had bought a load of cotton tops and little shorts that I hoped struck some sort of balance.

The first process of the packing was to put labels on all

of my cosmetics to cover up the names, as we weren't allowed to promote any brands that were not official sponsors. Then I had to pack everything I was going to need into the two suitcases provided. After that, we had to take everything out again. Then we had to line it all up and make a list of everything that was in the bag. This was so that if anything got lost, or if we left the house early and left anything inside, there would be confirmation that it was ours and we had brought it in.

Then, a second handler, who wasn't the one usually assigned to us (after forty-eight hours in the hotel we were becoming buddies), was sent in. We had to go through every single item on the list as we put it into the suitcase, to prove that everything was as the paperwork said it was. No products that were not specifically sponsoring the show, no illegal items, nothing against the rules, and no items in the case that weren't on the list. Boring. But then, when you've been to residential rehab – where they are literally taking your perfume in case of alcohol abuse and your shoelaces in case of suicide – it's not too bad.

The most boring thing about those two days at the hideout hotel was that we had no access to our phones or to the internet by then and we couldn't watch TV. I realised just how much I was used to looking at my phone! I chose to fill my time with getting as much nice food in as I could, as Heidi had warned me that I would not be eating much in the house, and that what I was eating would not be great. I made the room service menu my friend and committed to getting to know it as well as possible before leaving for the studios.

On the actual launch day of the show, they finally came and moved me from the hotel, and took me to the studios. As with any time they had led us around the hotel over the last couple of days, my handler turned up with a folded sheet to put over my head. By this point I had been leading such a weird, cut-off existence for a couple of days already that I had started to think it was perfectly normal to leave a hotel in central London with a sheet on my head and hop into a car heading for the outskirts of the city.

I had no idea who else might be going into the house that day – apart from one girl, Lauren Goodger from *TOWIE*. And that was only because I had seen her long blonde hair poking out from beneath her own sheet as she walked out of one of the hotel rooms earlier in the week – and because of the publicity surrounding the show before we had gone in. I had asked my handler if it was her, but she had just stonewalled me – they knew better than to start answering bored future contestants whose minds were running away with them.

When we arrived at the studios there were loads of different dressing rooms keeping us all separate. A sound technician came and talked to me about how to use the microphones – how to turn them on, keep them safe and change the batteries when Big Brother needed us to.

Then, for almost all of the rest of the day, I was left in that dressing room with little but my thoughts to keep me company. By now, because we were all so physically close to each other, the walkie-talkies of the handlers were bleating with conversation almost the entire time. 'Snickers needs to go to the bathroom,' 'Godiva is ready,' 'Can Gummy Bear get a coke?' That sort of thing. What I managed to work out by the time I was dressed and ready for the show was that Gummy Bear had a seriously tiny bladder and Ferrero Rocher needed a lot of hair and make-up attention. I found myself getting more and more bored. There was a sense of tension around me, but it seemed like the time for the show might never actually arrive. I was offered wine, but said no, thank you. The waiting had made me so nervous, just sitting by myself all day. I would have done almost anything to break up the tedium but I knew wine wasn't the answer – I wanted to be clear-headed when I went into that house.

Eventually someone came and explained the process of the live entrance show to me. Where to walk, where to stop and talk to the presenter Emma Willis, where to look for my friends or family, and when to head into the house itself. I got myself ready, and looked forward to seeing Lucy Watson, her sister Tiffany and my British agent Emily, who would all be in the audience to support me. It already felt as if I hadn't seen them for weeks!

When I was eventually taken to the car that would be

taking me to the stage area, my heart was hammering with excitement and nerves. The car itself did nothing to calm that – it had foil taped to all of the windows and music blaring inside of it so that I couldn't see or hear who else was being introduced on the stage before me. I was sat in the car, my vision all blocked and foil and towels everywhere, with my handler beside me, for what felt like hours. Every few minutes I would feel the hum of the engine and the car slowly move a few inches up in the queue of vehicles waiting to deliver the contestants. In the end I started to feel as if I were part of some sort of friendly kidnap: when would I be set free?

At last, it was my turn. Suddenly my handler's walkie-talkie activated, and she turned to me, saying, 'Go go go GO! GO! GO!'

I headed out of the car, and as I did I saw the person who I had signed all my contracts with. I smiled and waved, trying to say 'Hi' over the noise of the crowd, but they just shouted GO GO GO at me, and I turned and realised I was on camera already. I waved to the crowd and headed for the show . . .

In those few days before the show I had taped so much footage. All I really cared about was that I didn't say anything which would make the crowd boo at me, and it seemed to go okay, with no nasty editing surprises. When I met Emma I could barely speak as I was so bewitched by how beautiful her eyes were. I just wanted to stare and stare at them as she asked me some standard questions about my plans for the house and whether Heidi and Spencer had given me some tips. As I heard myself answering, I started to wish they had given me some more. This all seemed like a bigger deal than the fun summer camp I had let myself believe I was off to.

Eventually it was time to enter the house itself. I turned to wave at the crowd one last time, spotting Lucy, Tiffany and Emily just where I had been told they would be. Then I went up the steps and waited. Because I had thought that when you get through those main doors, there was going to be another car there, ready to take me to 'the house'. I had never realised that the house was part of the set itself, right there behind those doors. Like I said, I should maybe have researched things a bit more thoroughly – but life is too short for getting stressed about these things. I just had to find my way into the living room and get ready to meet people.

When I walked into the living area, the only person I recognised was film actor Gary Busey, who was easily the most famous person in the house, and also the only one I had met before. He had filmed something with my brother and we're all from Malibu, so I went up to him and waved.

'Hey, Gary,' I said as I approached him. 'It's Stephanie, Pratt, you know my brother Spencer.'

'No I don't,' he said. And looked away.

'Okaaaaaay', I thought to myself. 'This is going to be a weird one.' If only I'd known just how weird. Because he absolutely had met me before, in Malibu, and there was no reason at all for him to have shut me down like that. I was happy to start a shitlist, just to put him on it.

Introducing myself and being introduced to everyone else was pretty simple. I didn't really know who anyone was, but we were all in the same boat so generally people were quick and relaxed about giving their details. There were no uncomfortable 'Don't you know who I am?' scenes from anyone.

My instinct was to head to the women who were all in there already. Claire King from *Emmerdale* seemed lovely and I just thought that Kellie Maloney was a sweet, quite drunk, older lady. I wanted to take care of her immediately, and was absolutely oblivious to the fact that she had been Frank Maloney – one of the country's most intimidating boxing promoters of a generation – only a few months ago. The fact that she was transitioning passed me by entirely until about three days later. I immediately liked ex B*witched singer Edele Lynch, and had a great feeling that we'd become good friends.

When James Jordan arrived I assumed he was gay until I learned he was a professional dancer who was far from it. When ex-Gladiator David McIntosh came in I was mesmerised by his buff physique, and when Ricci Guarnacci from *Geordie Shore* arrived I immediately realised that he had been the 'Rolo' I had heard the handlers talking about, saying he was so much fun. As all the pieces of the *Big Brother* jigsaw started to slot together I began to think I would have more and more fun over the forthcoming weeks. The only thing I was a little disappointed by was the fact that I wasn't really attracted to anyone in there. No summer fling for me, I thought.

The atmosphere was pretty hectic in there that first night. I had arrived as one of the later housemates and by the time I had said hi to everyone and fancied a glass of something, all of the drink was long gone.

We were all quite anxious about where we would be sleeping by the time Big Brother opened up the door to the bedroom. The whole time we were being introduced to each other, there was an undercurrent. Who do I want to share a bed with? Does this look like someone I could share a bed with? Edele seemed really keen to be a friend so I went with it, thinking it was great that that was sorted.

We all ran in, desperate to get ourselves a good position or a single bed, so that we could have a tiny bit of control over our environment. I remembered being a teenager and watching *The Real World* as each year's intake would rush to the bedrooms hoping for a good spot. What a bunch of losers I had always thought they were. Now, I was sprinting to the double bed I wanted, wildly hoping I'd make it.

When we entered the room we saw that there were three

beds with names on: Gary, Dee (from *Benefits Street*) and
Kellie. The others were for the rest of us to sort out ourselves.
There was a huge bed next to the one that Edele and I had
chosen, a sort of 'princess and the pea' bed, and Lauren
Goodger sauntered up to it alone. Casually, she said, 'So I'll
just take this one then, okay?' and seemed to be hoping for
the best. Good for her, I thought, kind of admiring her bold-
ness. But things didn't work out, as moments later Audley
Harrison – an ex-professional boxer – realised that he would
not physically fit into any of the remaining beds.

'Can I take this one?' he meekly asked Lauren, who
awkwardly went off to bunk up with Claire.

The next thing was finding space for all of our stuff. On
that first night, we only had one suitcase with us each, and
it was the smaller one. It wasn't until the next day that
we were given our larger suitcases and the hunt for space
began in earnest. There really was hardly any shelf or
cupboard space. I didn't have a hanger the entire time I
was there! I found it really interesting watching how much
you could tell about all the different personality types by
how they handled this.

You could either get busy at this early stage and nestle
in, finding yourself space and comfort before anyone else
would step up for it. Or you could use that time for
creating bonds, and trying to get to know people. I most
definitely chose the latter. I couldn't be bothered to get
myself into tension over a cupboard on Day 1, and happily

just stacked my clothes up on the end of my bed each morning instead. I had to *beg* for a plastic bag to put my dirty laundry in, though, which seemed a bit much.

Soon the house fell into a rhythm of daily life, with each of us forming our little alliances and habits to help us get on with the time away from home. Big Brother would turn on the lights and try to force us up at a decent time in the morning, but we were left to stay up as late as we wanted at night. After a few days friendships tended to form according to who stayed up when. I was a pretty early riser, and as I didn't drink in there, I was happy to head to bed at about 11.00 pm. Others were staying up three or four hours later than that, so they weren't up for much socialising during the morning as they were nursing their hangovers.

That first morning I made eggs for everyone as I was one of the first up. I remember Edele coming into the kitchen area and seeing what I was doing, before saying, 'Oh, you're making eggs, are you? I am known to make the best eggs in the world.'

Another 'okaaaaaaaay' moment. Why be competitive over eggs? Surely lots of people can make decent eggs.

'Great,' I said, 'you can do them tomorrow.' I wasn't going to rise to that one . . .

It was interesting how much the hierarchy of the house settled around the kitchen and the food. It's not always the case, but I had assumed it would be women dominating in the kitchen. In fact, there was a weird sexism over the food from almost Day 1. Audley did most of the cooking. It was very much a 'my way or the highway' situation, within only a few meals. Audley was the big guy so he took control. He was nice, but it was frustrating. It was like someone had told him the person who cooks never gets voted out. And the men ate all of the meat and salmon, on the understanding that they needed the protein. Fair enough, but women need protein, too, and meat isn't the only place to get it. I felt several unwritten rules developing, which were never discussed but were nevertheless unbreakable – unless you wanted trouble.

And I didn't want trouble. I would often have entire days when all I'd eat were some chickpeas or kidney beans. Straight out of the can, as I perched at the kitchen counter. Then all I'd have to do was to rinse a fork. Because as well as the unwritten rules around the cooking there were just as many over the washing-up. If you were cooked for, you were expected to clean up. And the boys never cooked tidily – the kitchen was destroyed once they had finished! It was a delicate system of building up favours and needing to pay them back with chores, and it was a whole load of politics I did my best to stay out of.

I would much rather have cooked than cleaned! Cooking is creative and fun, and makes other people feel good about you. Cleaning up is boring and dirty, and everyone walks off and leaves you to it as they're not hungry and curious any more. But I have survived residential rehab. For months. So while I might not have had the best strategies for winning a game show, I really did know what I needed to do to keep the environment around myself as calm as possible. Especially as I became increasingly aware that people did have strategies to either get as much airtime as possible, or to win. How exhausting.

The main gang that I hung out with was James, George Gilbey from *Gogglebox*, and Edele. George is such a good guy – I loved every second I spent with him in that house. He was always in a good mood, always helping out, always kind and just seemed like the perfect human being to be with. He was not grumpy for one minute of his time there. He would be doing laundry, cleaning up, and managing to be smiling all the time but not be doing it with any malicious strategy in mind. He would do the kindest things for no credit at all. I think he's the kind of guy who would donate a million pounds to charity if he had it, and never give his name away on the publicity.

I liked him in a holiday romance sort of way. We spent so much time together that he started to feel kind of like my 'husband in the house'. For me personality is by far the most attractive part of a person, and he had that in spades. I found him really attractive, and we kissed while we were in there. I suppose now I can see that we would never be able to date outside of the house, though, as we live too far apart and our lives are too far apart. At the time, and just after I had left the house, I am not sure that I saw it that way though.

The person who I was surprised not to get to know more was Lauren. If you'd asked me beforehand who I would have expected to forge a real bond with, it would have been her. There was no animosity at all, but for some reason, while we were in the house we never really clicked. I think it was probably that we were working on two totally different time zones, like ships passing in the night. She was up drinking until hours after I had headed to bed, and was outside in the smoking area a lot. But with no drink I was in bed early and up early with zero hangover every day.

Consequently I was always up for more games and pranks in the mornings. If I could have requested anything before going into the house, it would have been for more tasks and games. We had no paper or pens, no playing cards, and absolutely no books or magazines. It was worse than rehab in the way it sort of forced us into self-reflection through boredom. There wasn't even a gym or an exercise area, which I had thought there would be. Lack of exercise does not work very well for me, and nor does too much time to think, but being clear-headed was a big help, every single day.

The self-reflection affected some of us worse than others. Someone like Frenchy, a star of Playboy TV, had done a lot of reality TV and seemed pretty savvy about it all. Plus, she was totally shameless about hiding food and water for herself all the time. She seemed not to realise that there were cameras on us the whole time, and she would always get busted . . . She was a lovely person but frustrating to live with – not that she cared.

Kellie did not deal with it as well, though, and she ended up being the source of some of the biggest fights. I guess so many years in the world of boxing, keeping a huge secret about your gender identity, would leave you pretty toughened up. Audley would tell us stories about how Frank was the most hated promoter on the scene and I struggled to reconcile that with the Kellie I saw in the house. She was trying so hard with her femininity, and Lauren would be helping her with her make-up almost every night. But then she had this really argumentative side to her as well – and you never knew when it was going to appear. James got in a lot of fights with Kellie, and Audley. There was some serious jostling for the position of alpha in the house.

Without a doubt my main problem with the entire show was Gary Busey. Every time I fought with him I thought I would leave. He should not have been in that house; he simply was not mentally stable in my view. And his hygiene was horrific. I saw him naked every morning. He would walk around the bedroom entirely without clothes, trying to find his one pair of dirty cargo pants.

I don't know if he was naked because he's from California and it's hot there and he was used to it, or if he was trying to be sexually provocative. But I know what it felt like. His bed was next to Lauren's and I would hear her at least once a day suddenly go, 'Stephanie!' and I'd turn round and see he'd just taken off his pants again. He'd stand up and walk around. He had no respect for anyone's personal space.

It became a game for us to try and push people on to his bed if we were winding them up. We would scream if we touched anywhere in the entire area. One time Lauren was drunk and she fell on to his bed and she was just so distressed. Oh God, it was horrendous. He was absolutely unapologetic. He didn't seem to understand. Just simple things that we were all trying so hard to do to keep on each others' good sides, he had zero regard for. He was on my bed clipping his toenails one day and did not see why that might be a problem.

'Gary, you need to wear clothes,' we'd say. And it would just make him really defensive. And mean. He had a very mean streak to him. He always said, 'I'm going to win this show, don't talk to me like that.' And he did!

Having disgusting hygiene is a really low tactic for getting your own space in an environment like that. It's literally a case of making people not want to be near you in a space where room to move is in short supply. He used his disgust-ingness to his own advantage and he enjoyed it.

After six days in the house Audley and James had to take him into the bathroom and make him shower. Out of consideration for the rest of us, they literally forced him in. They undressed him and forced him under the water. Then, once he was in there, he started peeing. His hygiene was a real problem. His argument was, he didn't bathe at home, so he didn't need to do it there. He was a fucking asshole.

If you went in the bathroom after him the floor would often be all wet and our instinct was to smell our feet to check if it was spilled water or pee. Admittedly, the house became disgusting within a matter of days anyway – the shower was constantly covered with a thick layer of grime, and the plughole was clogged with hair – real and fake – which prevented the foamy water from ever going down. But Gary was the main problem. We always asked James to try and talk to him, as he was sort of buddies with him. But trying to talk to him was almost impossible. The man lives in a world of his own.

When I argued with him, it felt good. I wish I could say I was traumatised by the conflict and yes – I would rather have avoided it – but I just could not hold it in any more and I needed that release. No one was as big a germaphobe as I was – some of the others in the house just thought it was funny. But I would be crying in the diary room begging for bleach after finding out what Gary had been up to from time to time.

I have no idea how he won. He constantly told us that it was in his contract to win, but I find that hard to believe. When we had eviction nights he would stay in his pyjamas because he was sure he wasn't going. I expect he was just teasing us as he was so damn crazy. But Gary was more unpredictable than anyone I've ever known – flitting between dark menacing moments where he was almost threatening us, muttering that we had no idea what he knew about us, and just leaping about doing bird calls. It seemed to me that he liked making us all squirm, that he liked intimidating the girls and that he liked us not knowing what he'd do next.

It wasn't distress making him behave in a crazy way, as was the case with people I had been in jail or rehab with. I had the impression he was doing it knowingly and manipulatively. He constantly said, 'This is like a hotel for me, with you lot running around after me.' He was a vile person with zero manners or empathy.

The rest of my time was not too bad at all, though. I missed friends and family, of course, but I had been living abroad for a while by then, and it was a really insulated environment which didn't let me think about them too much. I didn't bring any photos so I didn't let myself get too homesick. George and James did such a good job of being my family in there as well. They were both so comforting, and so lovely. They were basically like my brothers, so I had two big brothers instead of one for a while . . .

I wish things had not got muddled with George, though. It was a pretty humiliating situation. If Edele or George had left before me, I would have been devastated. I would have been wandering around the house for the rest of the evening saying, 'Oh man, the house is going to suck now, for the rest of the run.' And particularly if George had left first – I would have been lost without him. But neither of them turned out to care much at all when I left before them: in fact, they cared so little that the first thing they did was get into bed with each other. I was gutted when I heard about that. It felt as if they had both been waiting for me to go, rather than having the fun I thought we were having.

When my name was called on Day 19 and it was my time to go, I was ready to head back to the real world. All I really wanted was that I wouldn't be met with a crowd of angry booing, and thankfully I wasn't. The doors opened and I was greeted by a sea of smiling faces, much to my huge relief.

As I came down the stairs I saw some of Edele's family holding up signs of support, and I made a point to go over to them and say how much I loved them. Never mind that while I was telling them that, she was moving to sit on George's lap. I had been sleeping with her night after night for nearly three weeks and she was already planning who her new bed partner was going to be. I guess the whole thing had been a competition for her after all, and I had just thought I was making a new friend.

My exit interviews went by in a blur – including the bit when I fell down the stairs almost into Rylan's lap on *Big*

Brother's Bit on the Side! But afterwards I was told by the producers that a lot of what had gone on with Gary they had not been able to show on TV. And I was encouraged not to talk about it myself now that I was free from the house's confines.

'Are you *kidding?*' was my response. 'So it just looked as if I was bullying an old man in there?'

I was furious that my response to Gary's grotesque behaviour had been fair game, but not what he had done to provoke it. Apparently mental-health charities had been in touch saying that there was a lot of stuff the show should not be broadcasting. As I say, I was encouraged not to talk about it myself. But there was no way I was going to keep quiet about it.

I was – at that point – just glad to be able to say nice things about George in the interviews I had lined up. I had faith that I would be able to give my side of the story at some point. No one ever really gets away with these things entirely, and I consoled myself with the fact that I would never have to deal with Gary ever again. I was out of there, and heading towards a clean, fresh bed – alone.

Most people when they leave the *CBB* house are desperate to have some drinks and celebrate with friends. Not me. I wasn't thinking about partying or having something luxurious to drink. I just wanted to stay awake long enough to order some pizza. I borrowed a producer's phone to call my mom before leaving the studio area as I hadn't been given my valuables back yet, and then headed straight for the hotel which was close by in Elstree.

The feeling when I finally got into that hotel bed was the absolute best. It was so late, and I was so exhausted, but I ran myself a huge bath and then got into that clean, white, crisp bed, and lay there like a starfish, squealing at the luxury of fresh sheets and total solitude. Heaven.

I had kind of imagined that I would be free the next day, but I had been naive. It was a full day of press and interviews, all sitting in the same small hotel room. I wanted to roam around the hotel and have a huge breakfast or another bath. Or even to go outside for a while after weeks of being in an air-conditioned environment. But no, it was interview after interview – me singing George and Edele's praises as they cosied up to each other, while I remained none the wiser.

At the end of that day I was moved to the Haymarket Hotel in central London – somewhere even more deliciously luxurious. To my utter delight I was told I'd be staying there until the end of the show and a little bit beyond. That room made my day cooped up in Elstree all seem worth it – in fact, I found myself wishing I'd been evicted two weeks earlier so I could have enjoyed longer there! The bathroom was the best bit, with a huge flatscreen TV above the bath. The hours I spent in there, catching up with TV and gossip.

The first non-*CBB* person I saw once I was out was

Lucy. As soon as I could I was off to The Phene, her dad's pub in Chelsea, for a massive catch-up. All of my gossip, all of her gossip, and some food that wasn't chickpeas from a can. While I had been in the house I had kept a mental list of the places that I would go to once I was out. I would just sit quietly and think about them while I was feeling hungry, or just a bit low. The list was big – but not too big for me! After only a few days, I had been everywhere with my good friend Dominic. We went to The Wolseley, Nobu, Cecconi's, Hakkasan – the restaurants I'd been dreaming of. It was one of the best weeks of my life for food, and I was so happy to be enjoying time in London.

Loads of my friends from my time in New York with Simon a couple of years before were around, so I was hanging out with them and my *MiC* friends, and having a fantastic late summer. That first weekend I went to the newly opened Chiltern Firehouse, and then to The Box, the nightclub that famously doesn't let reality stars through its doors. (They have kicked both Lucy and Jamie Laing out in the past.) Turns out that if you go with a bunch of discreet New Yorkers, they let you in just fine.

As ever, I did not watch the show back, so I don't really know what footage of me looked like. I learned long ago that I don't like to watch myself on TV especially when it's been edited to cause drama on a show. You just can't think rationally about your own image, and you see things that other viewers never would. And I didn't carry on watching the rest of *CBB* once I was out of the house, so I only found out about George and Edele from looking online and being told by Lucy and my agent Emily. It was hurtful, but I decided not to give it another moment's thought.

Being discussed online for so many years should probably have toughened me up a bit more by now, but I still find it incredibly hard to see the raw anger and hatred that people can express. So often, when I get tweets that are cruel, I want to retweet them, or to answer back publicly saying, 'What is wrong with you?' so that the rest of my followers will give them a hard time. But now, I simply never look. I can't take it – and more importantly, it's not worth it.

The very few times that I have gone out of my way to reply to someone who has said something mean or disgusting, they have replied with a fan-type reply. 'Oh my God I can't believe you replied, that is so cool, big fan of the show,' or something similar.

It's all about attention, is what I have learned. Now that Perez Hilton no longer writes about me, and he has dipped a toe into the reality TV world himself with his own disastrous turn on *Celebrity Big Brother* this year, I can see clearer than ever that he is just a really unhappy man. Being cruel about other people must feel like it's taking away from the pain of your own anxieties, but it just isn't. I would be lying if I said, 'Oh it never hurts me these days.' When I see it, it still does. The difference is that I just don't look any more. It's not worth letting strangers hurt my feelings.

I headed back up to Elstree, to the studio, to watch the finale show and see Gary crowned the winner. Afterwards we all headed to the wrap party. I ignored George all night, and was disappointed that he never even tried to approach me or apologise in the slightest for the way he had behaved. And I was furious when I saw Edele, but just about managed to keep things civil. Lauren, Ricci, Frenchy and David had seen what George and Edele had done, so I hung out with them all evening, and had a great time celebrating our time in the house. Lauren, Ricci, David and I all headed up to a club in Essex after the party, and I stayed in Lauren's hotel room. Finally, we bonded once we were both out of the house!

The next day, I headed back to the Haymarket, where I had decided to keep my room on for a couple of extra weeks while I started looking for an apartment in London. My year in London had gone so well that I now had tons of friends from *Made in Chelsea*, as well as tons who were nothing to do with it. It was starting to feel like home, so it was time to make things more permanent.

And then I bumped into Lucy. Oh, Lucy Watson, she knows how to activate my curiosity . . .

'So have you seen the new guys they have for this season?'

she casually asked me over a cold, end-of-summer vodka soda.

'Um, no,' I replied. I wasn't really interested, so soon after getting my fingers burned on *CBB*.

'Oh, there's one for you,' she said, peering over her glass. 'Josh. He's hot. Blue eyes. He has a bulldog puppy . . .'

I just thought she was winding me up and asked her to send me a photo when she had time. Later that evening, my phone beeped as the photo arrived.

Butterflies.

Oh, he was my type.

'Good call!' I replied to Lucy. 'You're so right . . .'

Then I fired off an email to *MiC* congratulating them on their great taste in men. A week later, Sophie Hermann was having a Bavarian-themed party, and Lucy texted to let me know that she and her sister Tiffany were going.

'Josh is coming,' she added. 'Just so you know.'

I was plaiting my hair before you could say 'Heidi'.

14

I was really excited about the party, it looked like being a good night and I wanted to look just right for the Bavarian theme. I had no idea where to go though – where does one find 'German-wear' in London? I didn't have a clue, so I went where most party dilemmas are solved: Topshop.

I just went to the personal shopping department and begged for their help. They had random things in different departments that meant I was just about able to put together a decent outfit. It was a case of a little skirt from one range here, a white blouse from another there, and then . . . I asked for some suspenders. I had forgotten that in the UK 'suspenders' are what we in the US call 'garters', so the lady who was helping me thought I was really going all out with my look! But, eventually, we worked it out and I found a cool pair of 'braces' to finish my outfit off.

It was out of the question that I could just turn up alone, so I got Lucy and Tiffany to arrive with me as my wingmen. It was a really cool party and the whole gang from *Made in Chelsea* was there. I'd always wanted to go to Oktoberfest, and the party was pretty close to how I imagined that would be, with everyone entering into the Bavarian spirit – lots of pretzels and calls of '*Prost!*' as we toasted with our huge steins. The party was well underway, and I was wondering if I would meet Josh. The next thing I knew Spencer was walking over to me. Great. By now he was going out with Lauren Hutton, but she wasn't at the party. He started telling me how sad he was that Stevie and I had broken up, but that he had someone he'd like me to meet.

I laughed in his face. I was not interested in anyone he might want to set me up with. But then I saw him turn and call someone over. It was Josh. I had no idea that he knew him too. I could not believe it was Spencer introducing us, I was mortified, and felt as if I'd been put on the spot. The way you want to behave around your ex is not necessarily the way you want to behave around someone new.

I could tell Josh was nervous too though, so I took some comfort in that and just tried to ignore Spencer, as ever, and he soon got the hint. Josh told me was just back from

LA where he'd spent a couple of months. He also told me about his ten-week-old bulldog puppy Maggie and I asked if I could meet her.

'Why don't you give me your number.'

He called me two days later and asked me out for a day date, and the way we planned it, it was all about the dog. I wasn't sure if I really wanted a date that was totally focused around a dog but then . . . then I saw him with the dog.

The date seemed to go pretty well. The next morning he texted me asking if I wanted to go to dinner the following night. And so we had our first official dinner date that Friday at Gaucho in Sloane Avenue. From the minute we sat down, the evening flew by. We talked about a million different things over dinner, from conspiracy theories to living in LA and the three years he had just spent in Dubai.

After the meal we ended up going to the Goat, where they have a private bar called the Prayer Room. It's a kind of a friend-of-a-friend deal where you have to know the right guy to be allowed in. I love it, and we stayed there chatting until about midnight. We were right around the corner from my flat on the Fulham Road, just next to the Chelsea and Westminster Hospital, so Josh offered to walk me home. We entered the lobby of the apartment block and the concierge discreetly looked away as Josh kissed me for the first time.

The next morning I woke up to a text from Josh saying
that he'd had a great time, and inviting me to his house
to watch TV and to cuddle with Maggie. It felt great to
be on his huge L-shaped couch, with Maggie and heaps
of plates all piled up on us as we watched *Friends*, the
show that had been my solace in some of my darkest
times. I was just wearing a hoodie, jeans and some
Converse. For once, I felt happy and relaxed, instead of
trying to look good enough or be good enough. It was a
mellow night in, ordering take-out from Jak's, watching
TV and playing with the dog until I headed home at
bedtime.

We didn't have the 'are we girlfriend and boyfriend'
conversation until a bit later, but from that weekend
onwards, it was basically a done deal. There was still a part
of me that carried the scars of past experiences, hoping
that Josh wouldn't turn out to be just another guy who
wanted little more than a slice of celebrity life. But how
could I know? I couldn't. How can you ever know about
anyone? You can't. And I couldn't just stay inside, never
falling in love with anyone in case it turned sour. So I
trusted my gut instinct and went with it.

As far as I was concerned the only hint of awkwardness
was that one of the first people that Josh made friends
with in London was Stevie, my most recent ex . . . Honestly,
he'd been away working in Dubai for three years, and now
he was back it was my ex who was living with one of his

closest friends. But there was no malice, and both of them are such good guys that things moved on pretty swiftly.

After a couple of months I was spending pretty much all of my time at Josh's apartment. At his request, I might add! After Spencer Matthews' hurtful comments about me 'all but moving in uninvited', I was *way* more careful about making it very clear whose request it was when I stayed over. I had apartments in both London and LA by now, I didn't need to be tarred with the brush of trying to move into other people's homes again! But us spending more time together was most definitely at Josh's request. Within a couple of months I was only heading over to mine about once a week, but, mentally, I wasn't ready to give my own apartment up yet. I had been burned before, so I wanted to keep that safe space, that little bit of independence.

There was a problem with his apartment though, and it was making it harder and harder to spend time there: there was terrible construction work going on above it. It woke us up at 5.00 am every day and continued at volumes that would make your teeth rattle inside your head. His neighbour was on to his third refurbishment, and there was no sign of it ending any time soon.

After we'd been dating for about two or three months Josh announced 'I *have* to get out of this lease, it's absolute hell here.' I couldn't agree more. So it was this, rather than any hurry to move in together that led to me looking around apartments with Josh before the year was out. We never actually talked about moving in . . .

This didn't stop me offering my advice on what I'd like in an apartment though. We both fell in love with the new apartment the minute we saw it and the decision made itself. But I didn't know it would be 'our' apartment until Josh presented me with my own key at Jamie Laing's Twisted Christmas Party.

The day after that Twisted Christmas party we both flew out of London at the same time, heading in different directions: me to LA and Josh to Barbados. We were each spending Christmas with our own families, and then the plan was for me to head to Barbados for New Year and we would both spend January in LA. As Josh had spent time living and working in LA too, it wasn't entirely unfamiliar territory. We would each show each other the city as we knew it.

It is always so cool to go back to LA and spend time with my mom and dad, my sister Kristin, her husband and her kids, and my brother Spencer and his wife Heidi – just doing family things like we've always done. Catching up with friends, shopping at the Brentwood Country Mart and checking out all my favourite stores. And of course, cuddling up with Kiki on the couch and watching TV. Although London is definitely a second home for me, and I loved my time in New York, LA will always truly be home. I just love being there for the holidays.

As I headed to Barbados straight after the holiday, I felt a little bit nervous as I had only met Josh's parents briefly in the UK, and now I would be staying at their home. As my flight left the ground the excitement overtook that completely, and before long I was heading out of passport control to see Josh in his board shorts and colourful Ray-Bans, grinning like crazy. When we got to the house everyone was there to say 'hi'. It was perfect, a beautiful home and the dream holiday. On New Year's Eve itself we went to a party at The Cliff, an incredible restaurant with stunning views out over the ocean. The whole family was clapping and cheering around me as the clock struck midnight.

After a wonderful holiday, we both headed to Los Angeles where we spent our time showing each other around – my high school, where I had my first job, my favourite restaurants – and hanging out with my parents a lot. In turn he showed me all of his haunts from his time there.

We also drove to Santa Barbara to visit my brother Spencer and his wife Heidi. I think Josh was surprised at how normal they were! These days they live up in a beach house on the coast. When we got there Heidi had put a huge bunch of flowers in the guest room and she had printed out a photo of us from my Instagram, framed it and put it by the bed so we'd feel at home. That girl is too cute! We settled in down by the view with chips and guacamole, and some fancy tequila and later we headed for dinner at their favourite Mexican restaurant and then we caught a movie. The trip was only overnight, but it was the best: super-chilled, super-relaxing and non-stop laughs all the way through dinner. It literally could not have been more perfect. So much had happened with Spencer and Heidi over the years, so the fact that we were just sitting there laughing and having a good time felt almost unbelievable.

We returned to London to our new apartment and everything that 2015 was going to bring. I had a huge sense of calm and positivity for the future. This year has brought all sorts – the usual *Made in Chelsea* dramas – but also writing this book and launching my 'Malibu' swimwear range with South Beach. I got to wear it all the time when I went to the Bahamas for my birthday in April. Probably the weirdest part of that trip was swimming with the feral pigs on the famous Pig Beach. I loved piggy island! Josh and I had a mini-break to Rome last month where we were *such* tourists – it is such a beautiful city. And I'm so excited to be going back to another great city – Los Angeles – for the summer and sharing my favourite places with all my *MiC* friends.

As I'm about to get on my flight and head out there, I'm not sure what's round the corner for me, but what I do know for sure these days is that whatever life throws at me – good or bad – I can handle it. Hopefully Josh is as genuine as he seems. But you never truly know people do you? That's why no matter what you must always be in charge of your own happiness. Everything happens for a reason, you just have to keep the faith and trust the universe.

Index

Acknowledgements

My gratitude to my family and friends who stuck by me through these crazy times.

Thank you to my loving parents who taught me that I could stand up every time I fell.

To my big brother for his advice and support – you are without a doubt the greatest big brother a girl could ever wish for.

Heidi – thank you for always reminding me that I deserve the best and keeping me optimistic everyday. I love you.

Kristin – thank you for being a great role model! I'm lucky to have you as an older sister. I promise to be a great role model for your kids!!!

Lucy – thank you for making me feel welcome in London and being such a loyal friend. Not sure I could have survived all of these disastrous relationships without you by my side. Love you, Bub.

Gina and Alishea – you girls have been there from day one, visiting me in hospital rooms and in rehab. I could never fully express my gratitude for having such supportive and loving friends. You girls have helped me get to where I am today and I will never forget that it was with your help and friendship that I was able to grow. I am forever in debt, I love you guys more than you will ever know!

Emily – my wonderful, beautiful and hilarious agent. In all of my years of work and TV I have never had an agent so dedicated and driven. It took eight years to find you, and it was so worth the wait! Thank you for being a friend, a publicist and my agent! Remind me I owe you a raise!

A big thank you to everyone I have worked with over the years. I must say it is the crew of the TV shows that make it such an enjoyable process! My *Made in Chelsea* family has been extraordinary to me... and I am so grateful to be a part of the show and live in the greatest city in the world.

I would also like to thank everyone who helped with this book. I always dreamt of writing about all of my adventures, so thank you for making it possible.

My agents at United Agents, Matt Nichols and Ariella Feiner – thank you for all of your hours and help. Ariella – congratulations on your new baby!!

Everyone at Headline, especially Sarah Emsley, for

believing that my story could be inspiring for others and taking a chance on it.

Holly Harris – thank you for all of your help and time!

Emma Tait – you have been so instrumental in getting this book finished and I couldn't have done it without you. Thank you for working weekends and in the middle of the night, you were absolutely amazing.

Last and certainly not least, my dear Alexandra Heminsley – I remember our first meeting at the Goat like it was yesterday! Writing this book with you felt like reminiscing with an old girl friend. Thank you for your work and time spent on this project. But what I really want to thank you for is being so compassionate. Your kind words and hugs when I was remembering the tough times and crying over the bad memories meant the world to me. Your text messages checking on me were above and beyond. Thank you for being such a comfort and friend. I am so proud of this book and you have helped me tell my story in a way that I am proud of and not ashamed by. So, a million times over, thank you.

Picture Credits